Instant Pot Recipe Cookbook

Over 140 Easy & Delicious Recipes

By Sydney Foster

© 2018

Table of Contents

Introduction

Your life may be busy, but that doesn't mean you can't have tasty, home cooked meals. Your instant pot makes that possible by allowing you to cook meals in less time while still being full of both nutrition and flavor. It's a common misconception that the instant pot is made for large meals. Though you can make large portions and freeze them for later, the instant pot can easily be used for two people to get meals in half the time without sacrificing the taste.

Your instant pot will become the most useful tool you have in your kitchen. You can forget the stoves, oven, pans and pot. Cooking will be easier and twice as fun. For some people, an instant pot is all that they need to cook home cooked meals on a regular basis. In this book, you'll go on a culinary journey from home cooked favorites to dishes all the way from Asia and India to bring a little more spice and exotic flavor to your table.

Breakfast Recipes

Breakfast is a tough meal for anyone, but trying to eat healthy during breakfast is even harder. Your instant pot can come in handy at making quick and healthy meals that will give you the energy you need to get through the day.

Instant Porridge

Ingredients:

- ½ Teaspoon Ground Cinnamon
- 1 ½ Cups Rice Milk
- ½ Cup Buckwheat Groats, Raw
- ½ Banana, Sliced
- 1/8 Cup Raisins
- ¼ Teaspoon Vanilla Extract
- Chopped Pecans, Optional

Directions:

1. Star by rinsing your buckwheat before placing it in your instant pot.
2. Add in your banana, rice milk, cinnamon, vanilla and raisins before closing the lid.
3. The steam release needs to be closed, and manually set it for six minutes on high pressure.
4. When it beeps, turn it off and allow for a natural pressure release. This will take about twenty minutes.
5. Stir your porridge when the natural pressure release is over.
6. Serve warm and topped with nuts if desired.

Espresso Oatmeal

Ingredients:

- 1 ¼ Cups Water
- 1 Tablespoon White Sugar
- ½ Cup Steel Cut Oats
- ½ Cup Milk
- ½ Teaspoon Espresso Powder
- Sea Salt to Taste
- 1 Teaspoon Vanilla Extract, Pure
- Grated Chocolate for Garnish
- Whipped Cream for Garnish

Directions:

1. Mix your water, oats, sugar, milk, espresso powder and salt in your instant pot before stirring.
2. Cook on high pressure for ten minutes. Use a quick release, and then add your vanilla extract. Stir before covering your pot. Allow it to sit for five minutes.
3. Top with grated chocolate and whipped cream before serving.

Apple Crisp

Ingredients:

- 2 Teaspoons Cinnamon
- ½ Teaspoon Nutmeg
- 5 Apples, Peeled & Chopped into Chunks
- ½ Cup Water
- 1 Tablespoon Maple Syrup, Pure
- 4 Tablespoons Butter
- ¾ Cup Old Fashioned Rolled Oats
- ¼ Cup Flour
- ½ Teaspoon Sea Salt
- ¼ Cup Brown Sugar

Directions:

1. Place your apples at the bottom of your instant pot, and then sprinkle with cinnamon and nutmeg. Top with water and maple syrup.
2. Melt the butter in a bowl, and then mix together your butter, flour, brown sugar, oats and salt together. Drop by the spoonful's on top of the apples.
3. Secure the lid, and then cook on high pressure for eight minutes. Use a natural pressure release, and then allow it to sit for a few minutes in order to thicken.
4. Serve warm.

Chocolate Oatmeal

Ingredients:

- 1 Teaspoon Vanilla Extract
- 2 Cups Oatmeal
- 6 Cups Water
- 2 ½ Tablespoons Cocoa powder
- 1 Cup Almond Milk
- 10 Ounces Frozen Cherries
- Chocolate Chips for Topping

Directions:

1. Start by adding all ingredients together in your instant pot before stirring. Make sure the lid is set to vent, and then place it in slow cooker function for six and a half hours.
2. Stir before serving.

Almond & Coconut Risotto

Ingredients:

- 1 Cup Almond Milk, Vanilla
- ½ Cup Coconut Milk, Unsweetened
- ½ Cup Arborio Rice
- 1/6 Cup Coconut Sugar
- 1 Teaspoon Vanilla Extract, Pure
- 1/8 Cup Slivered Almonds, Toasted

Directions:

1. Click your sauté button, adding in your coconut milk and almond milk. Stir constantly as it comes to a boil.
2. Once it's boiling, add your rice before stirring again.
3. Close the lid, and then click the manual button. Reduce the cooking time to five minutes.
4. Use a natural pressure release for ten minutes. Release the remaining pressure with a quick release.
5. Stir in your sweetener and vanilla extract.
6. Serve topped with your toasted almonds.

Earl Grey & Rosewater Oats

Ingredients:

- 1 ½ Cups Brewed Earl Grey Tea
- ½ Teaspoon Rosewater (Can Substitute for Vanilla for another Taste)
- ½ Cup Steel Cut Oats
- 2 Tablespoons Sweetener of Your Choice

Directions:

1. Add your oats and early grey to your instant pot, and then put the lid on.
2. Cook using your manual setting for three minutes. Allow for a natural pressure release, which will take about five minutes.
3. Add your rosewater and sweetener, and then serve topped with milk of choice.

Ham & Egg Casserole

Ingredients:

- 6 Eggs
- ½ Yellow Onion, Chopped
- 1 Cup Ham, Chopped
- 1 Cup Cheddar Cheese, Shredded
- 4 Potatoes, Cubed
- 2 Cups Water
- 1 Cup Milk
- Sea Salt & Black Pepper to Taste
- Cooking Spray

Directions:

1. Mix your eggs, milk, salt, pepper, ham, onions, potato, and cheese together in a bowl. Whisk together, and then pour into an oven safe pan that's been sprayed with cooking oil.
2. Put the water in the instant pot, and then place your steamer basket or trivet inside. Add your pan in, and then cook on high pressure for twenty-five minutes.
3. Leave your casserole to cool after using a quick release.

Meat Soufflé

Ingredients:

- 3 Eggs, Whisked
- Sea Salt & Black Pepper to Taste
- ¼ Cup Milk
- 2 Bacon Slices, Crumbled & Cooked
- ¼ Cup Ham, Chopped
- ½ Cup Sausage, Ground & Cooked Through
- ½ Cup Cheddar Cheese, Shredded
- 1 Green Onion, sliced
- 1 Cup Water

Directions:

1. Mix your eggs, milk, pepper, salt, sausage, bacon, ham, cheese, and green onion together. Stir before pouring it into a soufflé dish.
2. Place your water in your instant pot, and then add in your steamer basket.
3. Add your soufflé dish, and cover with tinfoil.
4. Cover your pot, cooking on high pressure for thirty minutes.
5. Serve warm.

Blueberry Bowl

Ingredients:

- 3/4 Cup White Quinoa
- ½ Cup Apple Juice
- ½ Tablespoon Honey, Raw
- 1/8 Cup Raisins
- 1 Small Cinnamon Stick
- ¾ Cup Water
- ½ Cup Plain Yogurt
- 1/8 Cup Pistachios, Chopped
- Blueberries to Serve
- 1/3 Cup Apples, Grated

Directions:

1. Start by rinsing your quinoa using a fine mesh strainer. Add your water, quinoa, and cinnamon stick to the instant pot. Lock the lid and then make sure your vent is sealed. Manually set it for one minute.
2. Use a natural pressure release for about ten minutes before using a quick pressure release.
3. Remove the cinnamon stick and set your quinoa to the side in a medium bowl.
4. Add in your honey, apple, raisins, and apple juice. Refrigerate for at least an hour.
5. Serve with yogurt and blueberries.

Egg Bake

Ingredients:

- 6 Egg
- ½ Green Bell Pepper, Diced
- 2/3 Cup Hash browns
- ½ Red Bell Pepper, Diced
- 1 Tablespoon Skim Milk
- 1/3 Cup Cheddar Cheese, Shredded
- Green Onion, Sliced Thin for Garnish

Directions:

1. Dice your peppers and cook them with your hash browns using the sauté function for five minutes. Your bell pepper should become tender.
2. While cooking, whisk your eggs and milk together with a pinch of salt in a bowl.
3. Pour your eggs over your pepper mix, adding in your cheese. Make sure to stir to combine.
4. Seal the lid cooking using high pressure for ten minutes.
5. Use a quick release, and then plate with green onions for garnish.

Breakfast Quiche

Ingredients:

- 1 Cup Water
- 3 Eggs
- ¼ cup Milk
- 1 Tablespoons Chives, Chopped
- ½ Cup Cheddar Cheese, Shredded
- Cooking Spray
- Sea Salt & Black Pepper to Taste

Directions:

1. Mix your salt, pepper and chives together in a bowl with your milk, whisking well.
2. Wrap a cake pan in tinfoil, greasing it with your cooking spray. Add cheese to your pan.
3. Pour the egg mixture in next, making sure it's spread evenly.
4. Pour the water into your instant pot, adding your trivet or steamer basket now. Place the cake pan on top, cooking on high pressure for a half hour.
5. Serve warm.

French Toast

Ingredients:

- 3 French Bread Slices, Cubed
- 1 Tablespoon Light Brown Sugar
- 1 Tablespoon Cream cheese
- 2 Eggs
- 2 Bananas, Sliced
- ¼ Cup Milk
- ½ Tablespoon White Sugar
- ½ Teaspoon Cinnamon
- 1 Tablespoon Butter
- 2 Tablespoons Pecans, Chopped
- ½ Teaspoon Vanilla Extract, Pure
- ¾ Cup Water
- Cooking Spray

Ingredients:

1. Grease a heatproof baking pan with your cooking spray. Place a layer of your cubed bread at the bottom. Layer with banana slices next. Sprinkle your bananas with sugar.
2. Add your melted cream cheese, spreading it evenly over the brown sugar.
3. Add the rest of your bread, then banana slices, and then sprinkle with half of your pecans.
4. In a bowl, mix your sugar and eggs. Add in your vanilla and cinnamon, whisking until combined.
5. Pour this over your bread and banana.
6. Pour the water into your instant pot, placing your trivet inside of it. Put your pan on the trivet, cooking on high pressure for twenty-five minutes.
7. Sprinkle with remaining pecans to serve.

Breakfast Cake

Ingredients:

- 1 Cup Water
- 2 Tablespoons White Sugar
- 3 Eggs
- 1 Tablespoon Butter, melted
- 5 Tablespoon Greek Yogurt
- 5 Tablespoons Ricotta Cheese
- 1 Teaspoon Vanilla Extract, Pure
- 1 Teaspoon Baking Powder
- ½ Cup Whole Wheat Flour
- ½ Cup Berry Compote
- Cooking Spray

Ingredients:

1. Mix your eggs and sugar in a bowl, whisking until your sugar dissolves.
2. Add in your butter, vanilla, Greek yogurt, and ricotta cheese. Whisk again.
3. In a different bowl mix your flour rand baking powder together. Stir this mixture into your eggs, making sure it's well combined.
4. Pour this into your cake pan that's been creased with your cooking spray. Make sure that it' spread evenly.
5. Drop your berry compote into the cake mixture by the spoonfuls, swirling with a knife.
6. Add your water to the instant pot, and then place the trivet inside.
7. Add your cake pan, cooking on high pressure for twenty-five minutes.
8. Serve warm.

Breakfast Burritos

Ingredients:

- 2 Eggs
- 1 lb Red potatoes, Cubed
- ½ Teaspoon Sea Salt, Fine
- 3 Ounces Ham Steak, Cubed
- 1 Small Jalapeno, Diced
- 1/8 Cup Yellow Onion, Diced
- ½ Teaspoon Taco Seasoning
- ¼ Teaspoon Chili Powder
- ¼ Teaspoon Mesquite Seasoning
- Tortillas

Directions:

1. Start by mixing your seasoning, salt, and eggs in a bowl with a tablespoon of water. Beat until your eggs are scrambled.
2. Add your potatoes, onions, jalapeno and ham to the bowl.
3. Add a cup of water to the bottom. Add the trivet, and then place your egg mixture on the trivet. Seal and cook for thirteen minutes on manual high pressure.
4. Once it's done, allow for a natural pressure release.
5. Remove the pan from your instant pot, and then fill your tortillas and serve.

Pumpkin Oatmeal

Ingredients:

- 2 Cups Water
- ½ Cups Steel Cut Oats
- ½ Cup Pumpkin Puree
- ½ Teaspoon Allspice
- ½ Teaspoon Cinnamon
- ½ Teaspoon Vanilla Powder

Topping:

- 2 Tablespoons Pecans, Chopped
- 3 Tablespoons Light Brown Sugar
- ½ Tablespoon Cinnamon

Directions:

1. Mix your water and steel cut oats together in your instant pot.
2. Add in your pumpkin puree, ½ teaspoon of cinnamon, vanilla and allspice. Make sure it's combined, and then cook on high pressure for three minutes.
3. In a bowl mixing your brown sugar, ½ tablespoon of cinnamon and pecans together. Make sure this is combined.
4. Divide your oatmeal up between two bowls, and then top with pecan mixture before serving.

Jamaican Porridge

Ingredients:

- 1-2 pimento Berries
- 1 Stick Cinnamon
- ½ Cup Yellow Cornmeal, Fine
- ½ Cup Whole Milk
- 2 Cups Water, Separated
- ½ Teaspoon Vanilla Extract
- ¼ Teaspoon Nutmeg, Ground
- ½ Cup Condensed Milk, Sweetened

Directions:

1. Push the porridge button on your instant pot, setting it for six minutes.
2. Add three cups of water and a cup of milk to your instant pot.
3. Whisk a cup of water and cornmeal together until it's completely combined. Add to your pot, whisking until combined. Add your pimento berries, vanilla extract, cinnamons stick and nutmeg. Cover, cooking for six minutes.
4. Allow a natural release, and then add your sweetened condensed milk before serving.

Vanilla Quinoa Bowl

Ingredients:

- ½ Cup Quinoa
- 1/8 Teaspoon Sea Salt, Fine
- ¾ Cup Water
- ½ Apple, Chopped
- 1 Tablespoon Cinnamon
- ¼ Teaspoon Vanilla Extract
- 1/8 Cup Sweetener

Directions:

1. Add all ingredients together, stirring well. Clock the lid and lock it, turning it to manual pressure.
2. Select open minute of cooking time, and then allow for a natural pressure release.
3. Open the lid and serve warm.

Sweet Potato Hash

Ingredients:

- 3 Eggs, Large
- ½ Tablespoon Italian Seasoning
- ¼ Teaspoon Sea Salt, Fine
- ¼ Teaspoon Ground Black Pepper
- ¼ lb Pork Sausage, Ground
- ½ Sweet Potato, Cubed & Peeled
- ½ Small Onion, Peeled & Diced
- 1 Clove Garlic, Minced
- 1 Cup Water
- ½ Medium Green Bell Pepper, Seeded & Diced

Directions:

1. Whisk your eggs, salt, pepper and Italian seasoning together. Set it to the side.
2. Press your sauté button, adding your sweet potato, garlic, onion, sausage and bell pepper. Cook for three to five minutes.
3. Transfer to a glass dish, and then pour your whisked eggs over your sausage mixture.
4. Place the trivet inside of your instant pot, pouring in water. Place the dish inside and lock the lid.
5. Press the manual button and adjust the time to five minutes.
6. Use a quick release, and then let cool for five to ten minutes before slicing and serving.

Peaches & Cream Quinoa

Ingredients:

- ¾ Cup Half & Half
- 1 Cup Peaches, Fresh
- ½ Teaspoon Vanilla Extract
- 1 Tablespoon Cinnamon
- 1 Cup Milk
- 1 Cup Quinoa
- 1 Cup Water
- 1 Tablespoon Butter

Directions:

1. Add your water and milk to your instant pot. Add in your quinoa, sprinkling with cinnamon. Stir, and then cook on high pressure for four minutes.
2. Use a quick release, and then stir in the patches. Add your additional half and half, and then add your vanilla or cinnamon.
3. Serve warm.

Strawberry Cheesecake Quinoa

Ingredients:

- ¾ Cups Quinoa, Uncooked
- 1 1/3 Cup Water
- 1 Tablespoon Honey, Raw
- ½ Teaspoon Vanilla Extract
- ¼ Teaspoon Pumpkin Pie Spice
- ¼ Cup Vanilla Greek Yogurt
- 1 Cup Strawberries, Sliced

Directions

1. Add your water, honey, quinoa, vanilla, strawberries, yogurt and spices into your instant pot. Select manual and set the cook time for one minute.
2. Allow for a natural pressure release for ten minutes before using a quick release.
3. Fluff the quinoa before serving.

Squash Porridge

Ingredients:

- 3 Apples, Cored
- 1 Delicata Squash
- 1 ½ Tablespoons Gelatin
- 2 Tablespoons Slipper Elm
- ½ Cup Water
- ¼ Teaspoon Cinnamon Powder
- 1 ½ Tablespoons Maple Syrup, Pure
- ½ Teaspoon Ginger Powder
- ¼ Teaspoon Cloves, Ground

Directions:

1. Place your apples and squash into your instant pot before adding your water. Sprinkle in your ginger, cloves and cinnamon before cooking on high pressure for eight minutes.
2. Let your squash cool down, and then cut in halve. Deseed, and then place in the blender.
3. Add in your apples, spices and water, pulsing until smooth.
4. Add the slippery elm, maple syrup, and gelatin, continuing to blend.
5. Serve warm.

Cardamom Yogurt & Roasted Peaches

Ingredients:

Yogurt:

- 5 Green Cardamom Pods, Crushed
- 4 Cups Whole Milk
- 1 Tablespoon Plain Yogurt
- 1/8 Cup Sugar
- ½ Teaspoon Cardamom, Ground
- ¼ Teaspoon Vanilla Extract

Roasted Peaches:

- 3 Peaches, Halved & Pitted
- 3 Tablespoon Old Fashioned Rolled Oats
- 1 ½ Tablespoons Unsalted Butter, Melted
- 1 Tablespoon Brown Sugar, Firmly Packed
- 1/8 Teaspoon Ground Cardamom

Directions:

1. You'll start by making your yogurt. Pour your milk into your instant pot, and put your cardamom pods in a square of cheesecloth before also placing them in a pot.
2. Lock the lid, and make sure that your valve is sealed. Pressure the yogurt button until your screen says boil and cook. It should reach 180 degrees, which will take about twenty-five minutes.
3. You should have an ice water bath ready, and remove the lid. Remove your cardamom.
4. Transfer the inner pot to your ice water bath, and stir until it cools to 110 degrees, which should take about ten minutes.
5. Transfer your cup of milk to a bowl, whisking in your yogurt until smooth. Return it to the pot, adding in your cardamom, vanilla and sugar, whisking until blended.
6. Return the inner pot to your instant pot, and then lock the lid in place. Make sure to seal the valve, and then press the warm button to reset the program. Press the yogurt button, setting the

cook time to ten hours. Once your yogurt is ready refrigerate for about four hours. Do not stir.

7. Line a large fine mesh sieve using four cheesecloths, and place it over the bowl. Spoon your yogurt into it, and let stand in the refrigerator for two hours. Drain the excess liquid.

8. Prepare your roasted peaches by baking them in the oven at 350.

9. In a small bowl stir in your oats, butter, cardamom, and brown sugar, mixing well. Sprinkle it over your peaches and continue to roast for thirty to thirty-five minutes.

10. Serve over your yogurt.

Eggs en Cocotte

Ingredients:

- 1 Cup Water
- Sea Salt & Black Pepper to Taste
- 1 Tablespoons Cream
- 2 Large Eggs
- 2/3 Tablespoons Chives
- Butter, Room Temperature

Directions:

1. Wipe the sides of two large ramekins with butter.
2. Pour a tablespoon of cream into each, and then crack and egg into each one. Sprinkle with chives.
3. Place the rack at the bottom of your instant pot, and then add a cup of water in your instant pot before putting your ramekin on the rack.
4. Close, sealing the lid and then press manual. Adjust the cook time to two minutes.
5. Use a quick release, and then season with salt and pepper before serving. Some people prefer to serve with toast.

Easy Banana Bread

Ingredients:

- ½ Tablespoon Vanilla Extract Pure
- ½ Stick Butter, Softened
- ¼ Cup White Sugar
- 2 Bananas, Peeled & Mashed
- 1 Egg
- 1 Cup Flour
- 1 Cup Water
- ½ Teaspoon Baking Powder
- Cooking Spray

Directions:

1. Mix your banana puree with your butter, sugar, flour, vanilla, egg and baking powder in a bowl. Stir until combined.
2. Grease a loaf pan using your cooking spray before pouring your bread mixture in.
3. Place the water in your instant pot, and then put your trivet in it. Place the loaf pan inside.
4. Cook using high pressure for fifty minutes before serving warm or cooled.

Vegetable Casserole

Ingredients:

- 3 Eggs
- 3 Tablespoons Milk
- 3 Tablespoons White Flour
- ½ Cup Tomatoes, Chopped
- 1 Small Bell Pepper, Chopped
- Sea Salt & Black Pepper to Taste
- 1 Green Onion, Chopped
- ½ Cup Cheddar Cheese, Shredded
- 1 Zucchini, Chopped
- 1 Cup Water

Directions:

1. Mix your eggs, flour, salt, pepper, milk, tomatoes, bell pepper, zucchini, onion and half of your cheese in a bowl. Stir well.
2. Pour into a heatproof dish, covering with tinfoil.
3. Place your water in your instant pot, and then add the trivet.
4. Then add your dish before cooking on high pressure for a half hour.
5. Uncover, sprinkling with cheese, and then serve warm.

Spanish Potato Hash

Ingredients:

- 3 Potatoes, Large
- ½ Chorizo Sausage
- 2 Slices Back Bacon
- ½ Onion, Peeled & Diced
- 125 Grams Soft Cheese
- 1 Tablespoon Greek Yogurt
- ½ Tablespoon Garlic Puree
- ½ Tablespoon Olive Oil
- 100 ml Vegetable Stock
- 1 ½ Tablespoons Rosemary
- 1 ½ Tablespoons Basil
- Sea Salt & Pepper to Taste

Directions:

1. Place your garlic, olive oil and onion into your instant pot, pressing sauté. Sauté until your onions have softened.
2. Peel and dice your potatoes before slicing your sausage tin. Add these into your pot as well, cooking and adding more olive oil as necessary.
3. Slice your bacon into chunks, adding this to your instant pot as well. Add in your seasoning, cooking for a few more minutes.
4. Add in your stock, placing it on the soup setting for ten minutes. Make sure that you seal your valve.
5. Use a quick release, and then drain away your stock water.
6. Add a little more herbs and mix in a bowl along with your cheese and Greek yogurt.

Peachy Breakfast

Ingredients:

- 1 Cup Rolled Oats
- ½ Peach, Chopped
- 2 Cups Water
- 1 Tablespoon Flax Meal
- ½ Teaspoon Vanilla Extract, Pure
- 3 Tablespoons Almonds, Chopped
- Maple Syrup, Pure to Taste

Directions:

1. Mix your oats, peach, water and vanilla in your instant pot. Stir and then cook on high pressure for three minutes.
2. Stir your oatmeal before dividing between two bowls. Top with maple syrup, almonds and flax meal before serving.

Lunch Recipes

If you're worried about lunch, don't worry because your instant pot can help with some healthy and filling meals here too. Healthy lunches don't have to take hours to prepare.

Fried Rice

Ingredients:

- 1 Cup Long Grain Rice
- 1 Carrot
- 1 ¼ Cups Vegetable Broth
- 1 ½ Tablespoons Extra Virgin Olive Oil
- 1 Egg
- ¼ Cup Frozen Peas
- Sea Salt & Pepper to Taste

Directions:

1. Add your vegetable stock and rice into your instant pot. Make sure the rice is spread evenly throughout, and then dice your carrot and add it.
2. Seal your instant pot and using the manual setting, set it to three minutes.
3. Let sit, and then release the pressure manually.
4. Mix the rice, and then press the sauté function. Add in your frozen peas and oil, sautéing for another minute.
5. Make a well in the middle of your rice, and beat your eggs in a separate bowl. Pour your beaten eggs into the well, and then fry everything together for one to two minutes.
6. Season with salt and pepper to taste before serving.

Asparagus Risotto

Ingredients:

- ¼ Teaspoon Sea Salt
- ¼ Bunch Asparagus, Diced
- ¼ Fennel, Diced
- 1 Tablespoon Olive Oil
- ½ Brown Onion, Diced Fine
- 1 Large Garlic Clove, Minced
- 1 Cup Arborio Risotto Rice
- 1/6 Cup White Wine
- ½ Lemon, Zested
- 1 Cup Vegetable Stock
- 1 Cup Chicken Stock
- 1 Tablespoon Butter
- ¼ Cup Parmesan Cheese
- ½ Fennel, Sliced for Topping
- ½ Tablespoon Olive Oil for Drizzling
- Sea Salt for Topping

Directions:

1. Start by pressing the sauté button, and then add in your olive oil and onions. Cook until your onions are tender.
2. Prepare the vegetables, dicing them as needed. Add in the majority (3/4) your diced fennel and asparagus, and then add in your salt and garlic. Stir thoroughly.
3. Add in your white wine, rice and lemon zest. Make sure to stir to combine.
4. Add in your stocks, stirring and press the keep warm button.
5. Place the lid on, and then use the manual setting and cook for five minutes on high pressure.
6. Heat a tablespoon of oil in a frying pan over medium-high heat while your risotto is cooking. Add in the remaining fennel and asparagus, and cook for five minutes. Stir, cooking until golden brown. Drizzle with lemon juice before setting it aside.

7. Allow for a natural pressure release for two minutes before using a quick release.
8. Open the lid, and stir in your parmesan cheese and butter. Add extra salt and pepper as needed. Serve topped with pan fried fennel and asparagus.

Quinoa Salad

Ingredients:

- ½ Cup Quinoa
- 1 Cup Strawberries, Sliced
- 1 Cup Water
- 1 Cup Pecans, Chopped
- 2 Green Onions, Chopped
- ½ Cup Broccoli, Chopped

Dressing:

- ¼ Teaspoon Garlic Powder
- Drizzle Olive Oil
- 1 Tablespoon Balsamic Vinegar
- ½ Tablespoon Basil, Fresh & Chopped

Directions:

1. Place your water and quinoa in your instant pot. Cook on high pressure for five minutes.
2. Use a quick release, and ten fluff with a fork. Allow it to sit for ten minutes.
3. Add your pecans, onion, broccoli and strawberries in a bowl. Toss.
4. In a different bowl mix your basil, vinegar, and garlic together with your oil. Make sure the mixture is smooth.
5. Add this to your quinoa salad, and serve room temperature or chilled.

Swedish Meatballs

Ingredients:

- ¾ Cup Beef Broth, Low Sodium
- ½ Cup whole Milk
- 12 Ounces Cream of Mushroom Soup
- 8 Ounces Egg Noodles
- 12 Ounces Meatballs, Frozen & Fully Cooked
- ½ Cup Sour Cream

Directions:

1. Add in your milk, cream of mushroom soup, water and beef broth, and then add in your egg noodles.
2. Layer your meatballs on top in a single layer.
3. Use the manual setting, adjusting the cooking time to twelve minutes before sealing your instant pot.
4. Release the pressure with two minutes remaining using a quick pressure release.
5. Stir in a cup of sour cream, and then mix thoroughly before serving.

Mushroom Risotto

Ingredients:

- ½ Onion, Diced
- 12 Ounces Mushrooms, Sliced
- 1 Sprig Fresh Thyme
- 1/8 Cup Red Wine
- 1 Cup Arborio Rice
- 2 Cups Chicken Stock
- ½ Cup Parmesan Cheese, Grated
- ½ Tablespoon Butter
- 1 Teaspoon Olive Oil
- Sea Salt & Pepper to Taste

Directions:

1. Press your sauté button, adding in your olive oil. Once your oil is hot, add in your onions. Cook until they turn translucent.
2. Add in your mushrooms and thyme, cooking until your mushrooms have softened.
3. Add in your rice, mixing well. Cook until your rice is lightly toasted.
4. Pour in your stock and wine, mixing well before adding in your salt and pepper.
5. Close the lid, and manually cook setting the timer for seven minutes.
6. Use a quick release, and then add in your butter and cheese, mixing well.
7. Enjoy warm. If it is not thick enough, then cook on sauté for another two to three minutes.

Sweet & Sour Chicken

Ingredients:

- 1 Chicken Breast, Diced
- 1/8 Cup Ketchup
- 1/8 Cup Honey
- 1 Tablespoon Soy Sauce, Low Sodium
- 1 Teaspoon Garlic, Minced
- Pinch Sea Salt
- ¼ Cup Rice Vinegar
- 1 Cup Brown Rice, Cooked
- 1 Cup Broccoli Slaw
- ½ Tablespoon Sesame Oil
- ½ Tablespoon Rice Vinegar
- ½ Cup Pineapple Chunks
- 1 Tablespoon Cornstarch
- 1 Tablespoon Water

Directions:

1. Whisk your honey, ketchup, garlic, soy sauce, salt, ginger, and ¼ cup of rice vinegar together in a bowl.
2. Place your chicken breast into your instant pot once it's been cut into cubes, and then press manual. Set it for seven minutes, and use a quick release once it's done.
3. Meanwhile, take another bowl. Toss your sesame oil, ½ tablespoon of rice vinegar and broccoli slaw together before setting it aside.
4. Once your chicken is done and steam released, then put your instant pot on sauté. Add in your pineapple chunks. In a small bowl, whisk together your water and cornstarch. Pour this into the chicken mixture. Whisk and cook for two to three minutes.
5. Serve with brown rice and broccoli slaw.

Instant Goulash

Ingredients:

- 1-2 Cloves Garlic
- ½ lb Ground Beef
- 1 Small Onion
- 15 Ounces Tomato Sauce, Canned
- 15 Ounces Diced Tomatoes, Canned
- 1 ½ Cups Elbow Noodles
- 1 ½ Tablespoons Soy Sauce
- 1 Tablespoon Italian Seasoning
- 1-2 Bay Leaves
- Sea Salt & Pepper to Taste
- 1 ¼ Cups Water

Directions:

1. Start by turning your instant pot to sauté, and then add your garlic, salt, pepper, onion and ground beef. Cook until your meat has browned.
2. When it's browned, drain the fat. Add in your diced tomatoes, tomato sauce and Italian seasoning. Stir well before adding in your soy sauce, water, noodles and bay leaves.
3. Place your instant pot on manual and set it for high pressure for four minutes. Use a quick release once it's done. Take the bay leaves out, stirring well before serving. Many people prefer to top with parmesan cheese.

Spinach Dip

Ingredients:

- 3 Cloves Garlic, Minced
- 1 lb Spinach, Fresh
- 1 Tablespoon Olive Oil
- ½ Cup Chicken Broth
- ½ Cup Sour Cream
- 8 Ounces Cream Cheese, Cubed
- ½ Cup Mayonnaise
- 1 Cup Mozzarella Cheese, Shredded
- 1 Teaspoon Onion Powder
- ¼ Teaspoon Black Pepper
- ½ Teaspoon Sea Salt, Fine

Directions:

1. Push the sauté button and combine your spinach and garlic together. Cook until your spinach has cooked down, and then drain the excess liquid.
2. Leave the spinach and garlic in the pot, but add the chicken broth, sour cream, cream cheese, mozzarella, and mayonnaise and onion powder. Stir to combine.
3. Add the lid, and then set the timer for four minutes on high pressure using the manual button.
4. Do a quick release and then season with salt and pepper. Serve warm.

Crispy Potatoes

Ingredients:

- ½ lb Fingerling Yukon Gold Potatoes, Cut into 1 Inch Cubes
- 1 Tablespoon Ghee
- Sea Salt & Black Pepper to Taste
- 1/8 Cup Italian Parsley, Minced
- ¼ Medium Lemon

Directions:

1. Add a half a cup of water to your instant pot before adding in your cooking insert. Dump in your potatoes, and then press the manual pressure and cook for five minutes on high pressure. Lock the lid, and make sure that the valve is sealed.
2. When they're done cooking, allow for a natural pressure release which will take about ten minutes.
3. Turn your instant pot to sauté and over medium high add in your ghee. Season with salt and pepper, and then toss with juice from the lemon.
4. Serve with parsley after they're fried to the desired texture.

Enchilada Pasta

Ingredients:

- 4 Ounces Pasta
- ¾ Cup Broth
- 1 lb Ground Beef
- 6 Ounces Enchilada Sauce
- 1 Tablespoon Taco Seasoning
- 1 Cup Shredded Cheese
- ½ Can Black Olives
- ¼ Cup Sour Cream

Directions:

1. Brown your meat with your taco seasoning using the sauté function.
2. Add your broth, enchilada sauce and pasta.
3. Place the lid, and then cook on high pressure for four minutes.
4. Use a quick pressure release, and then stir in your sour cream.
5. Layer the cheese on top with black olives, and then garnish as desired before serving.

Cheesesteak Sloppy Joes

Ingredients:

- ¾ Cups Ground Beef, Cooked
- ½ Teaspoon Garlic, Minced
- ¼ Teaspoon Black Pepper
- 1-1 ¼ Cup Onion, Sliced
- 1/3 Bell Pepper, Sliced
- ¾ Cup Mushrooms, Sliced
- ½ Tablespoon Flour, All Purpose
- 5 Ounces French Onion Soup, Canned
- ½ Teaspoon Worcestershire Sauce
- 1 Cup Mozzarella Cheese, Shredded
- 2 Hamburger Buns, White

Directions:

1. Place all ingredients except for your buns and cheese in the inner pot, and then lock the lid. Select manual and cook for six minutes.
2. Use a quick release to get rid of the steam, and then add the cheese.
3. Allow it to melt before serving on your buns.

Chicken & Mushroom Stroganoff

Ingredients:

- 2 Boneless Skinless chicken Breasts, Cubed
- 4 Ounces Mushrooms, Sliced
- 9 Ounces Cream Cheese, Softened
- 5 Ounces Cream of Chicken Soup
- 1 ¼ Ounce Dry Onion Soup Mix
- ½ lb Egg Noodles for Serving
- Sea Salt & Black Pepper to Taste
- Fresh Parsley to Garnish

Directions:

1. Start by placing your chicken in the bottom of your instant pot. Add in your mushrooms and cream cheese. Mix before adding in the rest of your ingredients besides the parsley and noodles.
2. Use your slow cooker function for three to four hours on high, and then serve with parsley and noodles.

Buffalo Chicken Sandwiches

Ingredients:

- ¾ lb Chicken, Boneless & Quartered
- ¼ Ounce Ranch Dressing Mix
- 3 Ounces Buffalo Wing Sauces
- 2 Buns

Directions:

1. Place all ingredients except for your buns in the instant pot, locking the lid.
2. Use the poultry setting and then set the time for fifteen minutes.
3. Use a natural pressure release for five minutes before using a quick release for the remaining steam.
4. Shred the chicken, serving with sauce on the buns.

Paleo Chicken Lettuce Wraps

Ingredients:

- ¼ Teaspoon Ginger, Ground
- 1/8 Teaspoon Allspice, Ground
- 3 Teaspoons Garlic, Minced
- 1/3 Cup Onion, Diced
- ½ lb Chicken, Ground
- 1/8 Cup Coconut Aminos
- ¼ Cup Sliced Water Chestnuts, Canned & Drained
- 1/8 Cup Chicken Broth
- 1 Tablespoon Balsamic Vinegar
- 1/6 Cup Green Onions, Sliced for Topping
- 4 Individual Lettuce Leaves, Romaine

Directions:

1. Place all ingredients into your pot besides your green onions and lettuce leaves. Lock the lid, and set it manually to cook for ten minutes.
2. Use a quick pressure release, and then use a meat masher to break up the chunks of meat.
3. Spoon onto the lettuce leaves, and sprinkle with green onions before serving.

Paleo Vegetable Soup

Ingredients:

- 1 Cup Celery, Diced
- 1 Cup Tomato, Diced
- 1 Cup Carrot, Diced
- 1 Cup Sweet Potato, Peeled & Diced
- 1 Cup Onion, Diced
- ½ Cups Bone Broth
- ½ lb Ground Beef
- Sea Salt & Pepper to Taste
- ½ Tablespoon Parsley, Chopped & Fresh for Serving

Directions:

1. Add your ground beef and onions into your instant pot, and then use the sauté function. Cook until your beef is browned.
2. Add your celery, tomatoes, carrots, sweet potatoes, beef broth and salt and pepper into your instant pot.
3. Lock the lid and cook using the manual setting for ten minutes.
4. Allow for a natural pressure release for five minutes before using a quick release for the remaining pressure.
5. Top with parsley to serve.

Potato Soup

Ingredients:

- 1 Cup Yukon Gold Potatoes
- ¼ Cup Onion, Diced
- 2 Teaspoons Garlic, Minced
- Sea Salt to Taste
- 1 ¾ Cup Chicken Broth
- 3-4 Ounces Cream Cheese
- 1/8 Cup Cheddar Cheese, Shredded
- 1/8 Cup Bacon, Diced & Cooked

Directions:

1. Add your potatoes, onion, garlic, seasoning and chicken stock into the inner pot, locking the lid.
2. Choose your soup setting and adjust the time to ten minutes.
3. Use the quick release, and then hit cancel before hitting the sauté button.
4. Stir in your cream cheese, stirring occasionally for two minutes. It should be well blended when you're done.
5. Top with cheddar cheese and bacon before serving.

Root Beer Pulled Pork

Ingredients:

- 1 lb Pork Roast, Quartered
- ½ Teaspoon Garlic Salt
- Black Pepper to Taste
- ¾ Cup Onion, Diced
- 1/3 Cup Root Beer
- 1/8 Cup Ketchup
- ½ Tablespoon Lemon Juice
- 1 Tablespoon Tomato Paste
- ½ Tablespoon Worcestershire Sauce
- ½ Tablespoon Honey, Raw
- ½ Tablespoon All Purpose Flour

Directions:

1. Sprinkle your roast with pepper and garlic salt before placing it in the inner pot.
2. Mix all other ingredients together before pouring it over the roast.
3. Lock the lid and then place on stew for thirty-five minutes.
4. Use a natural pressure release for five minutes before using a quick pressure release for the remaining pressure.
5. Remove the onion and roast. Shred the pork, and some people choose to discard the onions.
6. Add the roast back to the sauce, and stir to combine.
7. Serve on buns or in tortilla shells over rice while still warm.

Hamburger Soup

Ingredients:

- 2 Teaspoons Avocado Oil
- 1 lb Ground Beef
- 1 Small Onion, Chopped
- 2 Large Carrots, Peeled & Sliced
- 2 Large Celery Stalks, Sliced
- 1 Cup Yukon Gold Potatoes, Diced
- 2 Tablespoons Tomato Paste
- 1 Cup Green Beans, Frozen
- 14.5 Ounces Tomatoes, Diced & Canned
- 3 Cups Beef Broth, Low Sodium
- ½ Tablespoon Garlic, Minced
- 2 Teaspoons Sea Salt
- ½ Teaspoon Black Pepper

Directions:

1. Set your instant pot to sauté, and then add in your beef and oil. Cook until your beef has browned.
2. Add all remaining ingredients, stirring to combine.
3. Lock your lid, and set on soup setting.
4. Allow for a natural pressure release once it's done.

Vegetable Lo Mein

Ingredients:

- 2 Cups Bone Broth
- ¼ Cup Coconut Aminos
- 4 Cloves Garlic, Minced
- 2 Inch Ginger, Peeled & Grated
- ¼ Teaspoon Red Pepper Flakes
- 1 Teaspoon Sea Salt
- ¼ Teaspoon Black Pepper
- 1 Bunch Green Onions, Sliced
- 2 Large Carrots, Peeled & Chopped
- 1 Cup Frozen Peas
- 8 Ounces Mushrooms, Sliced
- ½ lb Pasta
- 2 Cups Baby Spinach, Chopped Fine

Directions:

1. Add everything except for your spinach into your instant pot before sealing the lid.
2. Press manual and cook for two minutes.
3. Turn it off, and then allow for a natural pressure release for four minutes.
4. Use a quick release after four minutes, and then stir in your spinach.
5. Serve topped with green onions or chopped nuts.

Chipotle Beef

Ingredients:

- 1 ½ lbs Beef Chuck Roast
- 1 Tablespoon Olive Oil
- ½ Chipotle, Chopped & Seeded
- ½ Tablespoon Adobo Sauce
- 1 Teaspoon Cumin, Dried
- 1 Teaspoon Oregano, Dried
- 1 Teaspoon Sea Salt
- ½ Teaspoon Black Pepper
- ¼ Teaspoon Chili Powder
- ½ Cup Cilantro, Roughly Chopped & Fresh
- ½ Small Onion, Peeled & Quartered
- ½ Green Bell Pepper, Chunked
- ½ Cup Water

Directions:

1. Start by salting and peppering your roast.
2. Press the sauté button, adding in your olive oil. Brown the roast on all sides which will take three to four minutes per side.
3. Drain any oil or fat as needed, and then put your roast back in your instant pot. Spread the chipotle pepper, adobo sauce, cumin, salt, pepper, oregano, and chili powder over your roast. Sprinkle with cilantro over it, and then add in your bell pepper and onion.
4. Pour the water around the edges.
5. Close the lid, and put on high for an hour. When it's done, release the pressure using a quick release.
6. Let your meat rest for five minutes outside of your instant pot, and then discard the vegetables if desired. Reserve the remaining liquid.
7. Shred the meat, and then return to the instant pot with the liquid. Place it on keep warm until you need to use it. Serve on buns or in a burrito.

Tortellini Soup

Ingredients:

- 1 Carrot
- ½ Medium Onion
- 3 Ounces Chorizo Sausage
- 1 Tablespoon Olive Oil
- 1 ½ Cups Vegetable Stock
- 1 ½ Cups Water
- ½ Teaspoon Sea Salt
- ½ Tablespoon Thyme, Dried
- ½ Handfuls Kale, Fresh
- 4-5 Ounces Tortellini, Dried
- ½ Cup Cream, Fresh

Directions:

1. Wash, peel and dice your onion and carrots. Cut your chorizo as well.
2. Press sauté on your instant pot before add in in your olive oil. Add in your chorizo, onion and carrots. Sauté for five minutes before turning off the sauté button. Add in your water, stock, kale, tortellini and water together. Close the lid before locking it. Adjust the time cooking on manual for three minutes.
3. Wait ten minutes and then manually release the pressure.
4. Use the sauté button again, and then pour the cream in. cook for one to two minutes. Place the inner pot on a trivet to stop cooking.
5. Serve warm.

Dinner Recipes

Dinner is an important meal of the day, and often it brings families together. Though, it can also be a stressor if you live a busy lifestyle with little to no time. That's where your instant pot comes in handy!

Stuffed Peppers

Ingredients:

- 1 Cup Water
- ½ Cup Uncooked White Rice, Rinsed
- 2 Medium Bell Peppers
- ½ lb Ground Turkey
- 1 Egg, Beaten
- 1 Teaspoon Garlic Powder
- 1 Teaspoon Adobo Seasoning Powder
- ½ Teaspoon Sea Salt, Fine
- ¼ Teaspoon Ground Black Pepper
- 1 Teaspoon Oregano, Dried
- ½ Tablespoon Cumin Powder
- ½ Tablespoon Chili Powder
- ¼ Teaspoon Chipotle Chili Powder
- 1 ½ Tablespoon Green Chilies, Diced & Drained
- ½ Cup Tomato Sauce

Directions:

1. Rinse the rice, adding it to a mixing bowl. Add in your peppers after deseeding them.
2. Put the water in the inner line of your instant pot, and then set it to sauté mode. This will begin to heat up the water.
3. Add in your ground turkey, and then add all other ingredients to your bowl. Mix well.
4. Fill each pepper with the meat mixture. It should come a little above your pepper tops, but don't pack them too much. Place

them on the trivet in your instant pot. They should be above the water.

5. Put the lid on, and then cook it on high pressure for fifteen minutes.
6. Allow for a natural pressure release for ten minutes before using a quick release.
7. Remove and garnish with cilantro before serving.

Garlic & Lemon Chicken

Ingredients:

- 2 Teaspoons Arrowroot Flour
- 1/8 Cup White Wine
- ½ Lemon, Juiced
- ½ Teaspoon Parsley, Dried
- ¼ Teaspoon Paprika
- ¼ Cup Chicken Broth
- 3-4 Cloves Garlic, Minced
- ½ Tablespoon Butter
- 1 Small Onion, Diced
- ½ Teaspoon sea Salt
- 1 lb Chicken Breasts
- ¼ Cup Soy Sauce

Directions:

1. Push the sauté button, and then put your onion and butter in your instant pot.
2. Cook for five to ten minutes. Your onions should have softened, and combine the rest of the ingredients minus your flour. Cover, and then press your poultry setting. Close the steam valve, and then let cool completely. Release the valve, and then take off the lid.
3. Mix ¼ cup of soy sauce with your flour, and then mix it with the rest of the liquid.
4. Stir and serve warm.

Easy Pot Roast

Ingredients:

- 1 Medium Onion, Chopped
- 1 lb Beef Chuck
- ¾ Cup Beef Broth
- 1 Bay Leaf

Directions:

1. Start by patting your roast dry, and season it with your favorite seasoning.
2. Place your oil in a pot, and then set to sauté. Brown your roast on all sides, and then remove the roast. Add in your broth, bay leaf and onions. Place the roast on top, and then cover and seal.
3. Use the manual setting, setting for forty minutes.
4. Use a quick release, and then strain the bay leaf out of your juices. Thicken juices with a slurry if desired.

Easy BBQ Ribs

Ingredients:

- 1 Slab Ribs
- ½ Cup BBQ Sauce, Divided
- Sea Salt & Pepper to Taste
- ¼ Cup Chili Powder
- ¼ Cup Water

Directions:

1. Start by wrapping a baking sheet in foil, sprinkling your ribs with chili powder. Season with salt and pepper to taste, and then add your water to the instant pot.
2. Add in your ribs, pouring ¼ Cup of BBQ sauce over them. Lock the lid, sealing the vent.
3. Press your manual button and then increase the cooking time to a half hour.
4. Use a quick release, and then serve warm.

Meatballs with Japanese Gravy

Ingredients:

Meatballs:

- ½ lb Ground Turkey Meat
- 1 Tablespoon Cilantro, Fresh & Chopped
- ¼ Long Red Chili, Diced Fine
- ¼ Teaspoon White Pepper
- ¼ Teaspoon Sea Salt, Fine
- 1/3 Teaspoon Onion Powder
- ½ Tablespoon Tamari
- 1 Teaspoon Sesame Oil

Sauce:

- ¼ Brown Onion, Finely Chopped
- ½ Tablespoon Coconut Oil
- 1 Large Clove Garlic, Grated
- ½ Cup Chicken Stock
- ½ Teaspoon Ginger, Grated
- 1 ½ Tablespoons Tamari
- ½ Teaspoon Fish Sauce
- 1 ½ Tablespoons Lime Juice
- ½ Teaspoon Sesame Oil
- 1 Tablespoon Mirin
- ½ Tablespoon Honey
- ½ Tablespoon Tapioca Starch
- Sesame Seeds to Garnish

Directions:

1. Add all of your meatball ingredients together in a bowl, mixing by hand. Roll into small meatballs, and then set it to the side. It will be easier if you wet your hands first.
2. Press the sauté button, and add the coconut oil and onion together. Cook for three to four minutes or until your onions

have softened slightly. Add in your ginger and garlic, stirring for half a minute. Turn your sauté off.

3. Combine your tamari, fish sauce, chicken stock, lime juice, sesame oil, mirin and honey together, whisking well. Add this to the onions, garlic and ginger in a pot. Add the meatballs, and stir until they're coated in the sauce.

4. Place the lid on, and cook on high pressure for seven minutes.

5. Let it release pressure naturally for two to three minutes, and then use the quick release.

6. Press sauté again, and cook while stirring frequently for six to seven minutes. The sauce should become glossy and begin to thicken.

7. Add a few tablespoons of the sauce into a bowl, whisking with your tapioca starch until dissolved. Return this slurry to your pot, mixing all the way through. This will thicken the rest of your sauce into a gravy.

8. Serve sprinkled with sesame seeds over white or brown rice.

Shrimp Scampi Paella

Ingredients:

- ½ lb Frozen Shrimp, Shell & Tail on
- ½ Cup Jasmine Rice
- 1/8 Cup Butter
- 1/8 Cup Parsley, Chopped & Fresh
- ½ Teaspoon Sea Salt, Fine
- 1/8 Teaspoon Black Pepper
- Pinch Crushed Red Pepper to Taste
- ½ Medium Lemon, Juiced
- Small Pinch Saffron
- 2/3 Cup Chicken Broth
- 2 Cloves Garlic, Minced or Pressed
- Grated Parmesan to Garnish

Directions:

1. Place all of your ingredients in a pressure cooker, layering your frozen shrimp on top.
2. Secure the lid, and then cook on high pressure for five minutes.
3. Use the quick release, and you should serve with rice. You can serve with shells on or discarded, but most people prefer to gently peel the shrimp at this stage.
4. Serve garnish with cheese.

Osso Buco Rice

Ingredients:

- 2 Lamb Shanks
- ½ Tablespoon Coconut Oil
- Sea Salt & Pepper to taste
- 1 Small Carrot, Diced
- 1 Small Onion, Diced
- 1 Small Celery Stick, Diced
- 1 Teaspoon Coconut Oil
- 1 Clove Garlic, Minced
- 1/6 Cup Red Wine
- 1 Bay Leaf
- 1 Tablespoon Parsley, Chopped
- 1 Cup Chicken Stock
- ½ Cup Tomatoes, Chopped
- ½ Tablespoon Tamari
- ½ Cup Basmati Rice, Uncooked

Gremolata:

- 2 Tablespoons Parsley, Chopped
- 1 Clove Garlic, Grated
- ½ Lemon, Zested

Directions:

1. Use a paper towel to pat your meat dry, seasoning with salt and pepper.
2. Add your coconut oil to your instant pot, pressing sauté. Once it's hot, add in your lamb. Pan fry for about a half a minute on each side to seal.
3. Remove your shanks, placing them on a plate.
4. Add your carrot, celery, onion and another half teaspoon of coconut oil, salt and pepper to your instant pot. Stir a few times and cook for five minutes.
5. Add in your red wine, and stir for thirty seconds. Add the rest of your ingredients except for your rice. Mix well. Return your meat

to the instant pot, placing it under the sauce. Vegetables should be above and in-between your pieces of meat. Stop your statue process.

6. Place the lid on, and then cook on high pressure for forty-five minutes.

7. Soak your rice for forty-five minutes, and then rinse. Place in a sleeve to strain.

8. Use a natural pressure release for five minutes before using a quick release.

9. Remove the bigger pieces of meat, putting them on a plate.

10. Add your uncooked rice, and stir. Place your meat on the top again, and then allow to submerge a little.

11. Lock the lid, and press your rice function. If you do not have a rice function, place on normal for ten minutes.

12. To prepare your gremolata, mix all ingredients together.

13. Allow for a natural pressure release for five minutes before using a quick release.

14. Open, and serve topped with your gremolata while still warm.

Jalapeno Popper Chili

Ingredients:

- ¾ Cup Onion, Diced
- 1/3 Cup Jalapeno, Diced & Seeded
- 1 ½ Teaspoons Garlic, Minced
- 1 ½ Cups Chicken, Cooked & Diced
- 1 Teaspoon Chili Powder
- ½ Teaspoon Cumin
- 1/8 Teaspoon Sea Salt, Fine
- ½ Teaspoon Oregano, Dried
- 1/8 Teaspoon Black Pepper
- 1 Cup Chicken Broth
- 5 ounces Diced Tomatoes with Chiles
- 7 Ounces Whole Kernel Corn, Canned
- ½ Cup Bacon, Cooked & Diced
- 4 Ounces Cream Cheese
- 1/8 Cup Pepper Jack Cheese, Shredded for Topping

Directions:

1. Combine your jalapeno, garlic, chicken, onions, cumin, salt, pepper, chili powder, chicken broth, oregano, corn and diced tomatoes together. Lock and cover, and then choose the soup setting. Adjust the cook time to ten minutes.
2. Use a quick release for the pressure, and then stir in your cream cheese and half of your cooked bacon.
3. Serve topped with cheese and the remaining bacon.

Stuffed Eggplant

Ingredients:

- 4 Small Baby Eggplants
- ½ Medium Onion, Chopped Fine
- ½ Teaspoon Ginger
- ½ Teaspoon Garlic, Grated
- ½ Teaspoon Red Chili Powder
- ¼ Teaspoon Turmeric Powder
- ½ Teaspoon Garam Masala Powder
- ½ Teaspoon Cumin Powder
- ½ Tablespoon Coconut, Grated
- ½ Teaspoon Brown Sugar
- ½ Teaspoon Sea Salt, Fine
- ½ Teaspoon Mustard Seeds
- Cilantro to Garnish

Directions:

1. Start by washing and trimming the stems from your eggplants. Leave about a half inch of each stem. Make a slit going almost to the end.
2. To make your stuffing mix your ginger, garlic, red chili powder, onion garam masala, turmeric, cumin powder, brown sugar, coconut, and salt in a bowl. Mix everything together, stuffing your eggplants with them.
3. Turn your instant pot to sauté, and then add your oil and mustard seeds. Let them crackle, and then add them to your stuffed eggplants. Add a half a cup of water, and then close the lid.
4. Set to low pressure for four minutes followed by a quick release.
5. Garnish with cilantro before serving.

Asian Sesame Chicken

Ingredients:

Sauce:

- ¼ Cup Water
- ¼ Cup Ketchup
- 1/8 Cup Soy Sauce
- 1 Tablespoons Honey
- 1 Tablespoons Sesame Oil
- ½ Teaspoon Rice Wine Vinegar
- ½ Teaspoon Ginger, Minced

Chicken:

- 1 Large Chicken Breast, Diced

Thickening:

- 1/2 Tablespoons Cornstarch
- 1 ½ Tablespoons Water

Directions:

1. You'll start by combining all of your sauce ingredients together in a bowl.
2. Place your chicken in your instant pot, pouring the sauce over it. Mix to combine, and then cook for five minutes using the manual setting.
3. Use a quick release to release pressure and then press the sauté button.
4. Mix your cornstarch and water together in a small bowl, and then add it into your pot. Stir well and allow to cook for one to two minutes.
5. Serve warm.

Shredded Venezuelan Beef

Ingredients:

- 1 lb Flank Steak, Cut into 2 pieces
- 1 Clove Garlic, Minced
- 1 Onion, Sliced
- ½ Red Pepper, Sliced
- 1 ½ Tomatoes, Sliced
- 2 Cups Beef Stock
- 1 Teaspoon Worcestershire Sauce
- ½ Tablespoons Tomato Paste
- ½ Teaspoon Cumin
- 1/8 Cup Ketchup
- ½ Tablespoon Olive Oil
- Sea Salt & Black Pepper to Taste

Directions:

1. Season your steak with salt and pepper and minced garlic.
2. Chop your onion, and lace your beef and onion in your instant pot. Cook for twenty minutes on high pressure, and then use a quick release.
3. Remove the beef, but save one cup of the stock. Place it to the side.
4. Shred your beef, and then cook for another ten minutes.
5. Press your sauté button, and then add in your olive oil.
6. Add in your pepper, tomatoes, and sliced onion. Cook until tender, and then add your shredded beef back in.
7. Pour ¾ of your stock back in with your Worcestershire, tomato paste, cumin and ketchup. If the sauce seems to dry, add more stock.
8. Season with salt and pepper before serving.

Moo Goo Gai Pan

Ingredients:

- ½ lb Chicken Thighs, Boneless & Skinless Cut into Pieces
- ½ Tablespoon Olive Oil
- ½ Cup Chicken Stock
- ¾ Tablespoon Soy Sauce
- ½ Tablespoon Dry Sherry
- ½ Tablespoon Cornstarch
- ½ Inch Piece Ginger, Peeled & Grated
- 1 Small Carrot, Peeled & Sliced Thin
- 1 Clove Garlic, Minced
- 4 Ounces Button Mushrooms, Sliced
- ½ Cup Snow Peas
- 4 Ounces Bamboo Shoots, Canned
- 4 Ounces Water Chestnuts, Canned

Directions:

1. Start by preparing your chicken thighs, and then chop your vegetables, ginger and garlic.
2. Turn your instant pot to sauté, and then add a half tablespoon of oil to coat the bottom.
3. Brown your chicken thigh meat for one minute. Turn off the sauté function.
4. Add half of your chicken stock, and lock the lid. Cook for one minute on high pressure, and then mix the remaining chicken broth with your cornstarch, dry sherry and soy sauce.
5. Allow for a natural pressure release for seven minutes before using a quick release.
6. Add in your ginger, garlic and liquid into your cooking pot. Sauté for one minute.
7. Add in your carrots and mushrooms, cooking for two minutes while stirring
8. Add your reaming vegetables, cooking for one to two minutes before serving warm over rice.

Tofu & Pineapple Curry

Ingredients:

- 100 Grams Tofu, Extra Firm & Cubed
- 1/6 Cup Pineapple Cubes, Canned
- 1/8 Cup Cashews, Raw
- 7 Ounces Coconut Milk, Canned
- 1 Tablespoon + ½ Teaspoon Thai Red Curry Paste
- ¼ Cup Water
- 1 ½ Tablespoons Peanut Better
- ½ Tablespoon Olive Oil
- 1 Red Chili, Dried & Broken into Pieces
- ½ Small Onion, Chopped
- 1 Teaspoon Garlic, Grated
- 1 Teaspoon Ginger, Grated
- ½ Teaspoon Soy Sauce
- 1 ½ Teaspoon Rice Vinegar
- ½ Teaspoon Coconut Sugar
- 1 Teaspoon Sriracha
- ¼ Teaspoon Turmeric Powder
- Sea Salt & Pepper to Taste
- Juice of 1 Small Lime

Directions:

1. Start by pressing your sauté button, and then heat up your olive oil. Add your dried red chili.
2. Add your onion, sautéing for a minute, and then add in your cashews. Cook until they change color. Add in your garlic and ginger, cooking until aromatic.
3. In a bowl whisk together your coconut milk, Thai red curry paste, peanut butter and water.
4. Add this mixture to your ginger and garlic, stirring well.
5. Add in your soy sauce, sriracha, rice vinegar, turmeric powder, coconut sugar and salt, stirring to combine.

6. Add in your cubed tofu, and then mix.
7. Cover and cancel your sauté mode. Press the manual button, cooking on high pressure for two minutes.
8. Use the quick release, and then use your keep warm button before pressing sauté again.
9. Add in your pineapple, allowing to simmer for one to two minutes.
10. Squeeze in your lime juice, garnishing with cilantro before serving over rice.

Beef & Mushroom Stew

Ingredients:

- ½ Tablespoon Olive Oil
- 1 lb Beef Chuck, Cut Into 1 Inch Cubes
- 1 Sprig Rosemary, Chopped
- ½ Medium Red Onion, Diced Roughly
- ½ Celery Stalk, Cut into ½ Inch Slices
- ¼ Cup Red Wine, Non Sweet
- ½ Cup Beef Stock, Salt Free
- ½ Teaspoon Sea Salt, Fine
- ¼ Teaspoon Black Pepper
- ½ Ounce Porcini Mushrooms, Dried & Rinsed
- 1 Large Carrot, Sliced into ½ Inch Rounds
- 1 Tablespoon Butter, Unsalted
- 1 Tablespoon All Purpose Flour

Directions:

1. Start by pressing sauté on your instant pot, and then add your olive oil.
2. Sear your beef cubes for about five minutes on one side.
3. Add in your onion, celery, rosemary, stock, salt, pepper and red wine. Mix together, and then sprinkle the mushrooms and carrots on top.
4. Close the lid and cook on high pressure for fifteen minutes. Use a natural pressure release.
5. While this is cooking melt your butter in a pan, and drizzle with flour.
6. Mix into a paste, letting it cook until your butter begins to bubble in the flour.
7. Remove the lid when it's done, and add six tablespoons of the cooking liquid into your flour paste. Mix well, and then pour back into your instant pot.
8. Bring it to a boil using sauté mod, and let it simmer until thickened. This should take about five minutes.
9. Serve warm.

Italian Beef

Ingredients:

- 1 Tablespoon olive Oil
- 1.5 lbs Beef Roast
- 6 Ounce Jar of Pepperoncini
- 1 Tablespoon Minced Garlic
- 1 Cup Beef Broth

Directions:

1. Use the sauté function, browning your roast on each side using the olive oil.
2. Chop the stems off of your pepperoncini, reserving the liquid.
3. Turn off the pot, adding your garlic, peppers and beef broth. Add about half of the liquid from your pepper jar.
4. Close the lid, and then seal your instant pot. Press the stew button, and set the time for 120 minutes.
5. Use a natural pressure release for ten minutes before using a quick release.
6. Remove the peppers from the pot, and then take the beef out to shred it.
7. Pour the juice from the pot in a different bowl. Serve with your Italian beef sandwiches.

Salmon with Chili Lime Sauce

Ingredients:

Salmon:

- 2 Salmon Fillets, 5 Ounces Each
- 1 Cup Water
- Sea Salt & Black Pepper to Taste

Chili Lime Sauce:

- 1 Jalapeno, Seeds Removed & Diced
- 1 Lime, Juiced
- 2 Cloves Garlic, Minced
- 1 Tablespoon Olive Oil
- 1 Tablespoon Honey, Raw
- 1 Tablespoon Hot Water
- ½ Teaspoon Paprika
- ½ Teaspoon Cumin
- 1 Tablespoon Parsley, Fresh & Chopped

Directions:

1. Combine all of your sauce ingredients together, and then set it to the side.
2. Add your water the pressure cooker, placing your fillets on the steam rack. Season your fillets with salt and pepper.
3. Cover, locking the lid and select the steam mode. You'll need to adjust the cooking time to five minutes using high pressure.
4. Use a quick release once it's finished, and then open the lid. Serve with lime sauce.

Pad Thai Pot

Ingredients:

- 1 Teaspoon Sesame Oil
- ½ Tablespoon Garlic, Minced
- ½ Teaspoon Grated Ginger, Fresh
- ¼ Onion, Sliced
- ½ Package Extra Firm Tofu, Cubed
- 1 Egg
- 2 Tablespoons Rice Vinegar
- 2 Tablespoons Soy Sauce
- 1/6 Cup Honey, Raw
- 1 Small Zucchini, Diced
- 1 Carrot, Cut into Sticks
- 1 Bell Pepper, Sliced
- ½ Package Rice Noodles
- 1 Cup Vegetable Stock
- 1/8 Cup Basil, Chopped
- ¼ Teas Crushed Red Pepper (Optional)
- Cilantro for Garnish

Directions:

1. Put your instant pot on sauté, adding your sesame oil. Once your oil is hot add in your ginger, onions and garlic. Sauté for about a minute.
2. Mix your tofu, and then put it to the side. Add in your egg, scrambling it. It's okay if some of the onion or tofu get in your egg during the scrambling process. Once it's completely scrambled, mix in the rest of your onion and egg.
3. Mix in your aminos, honey and rice vinegar. Add in your bell peppers, carrots and zucchini. Place the rice noodles in your instant pot, and pour your stock over it.
4. Push the vegetables and tofu to the side so that your noodles can be in the broth.

5. Add the lid, and then seal. Use your manual setting to cook using high pressure for three minutes. Allow for a natural pressure release, and then mix in your red peppers and basil.
6. Serve garnished with cilantro.

Mongolian Beef

Ingredients:

- ¾ lb Flank Steak, Sliced
- 1/8 Cup Cornstarch
- 1 Tablespoon Olive Oil
- ¼ Teaspoon Ginger, Minced
- 1/3 Cups Soy Sauce
- 1/3 Cup Brown Sugar, Packed
- ¼ Cup Carrot, Grated
- 1/8 Cup Green Onions, Sliced

Directions:

1. Start by coating your flank steak with your cornstarch.
2. Combine your soy sauce, olive oil, ginger, water, brown sugar, carrots, and green onions together before putting it in your inner pot.
3. Place your flank steak on top.
4. Lock the lid, and then set on manual for thirty to thirty-five minutes depending on how you like your steak.
5. Use a natural release for five minutes before using a quick release for the remaining pressure.

Cream Cheese Chicken

Ingredients:

- ½ lb Chicken, Boneless
- 1/3 Ounce Italian Dressing Dry Mix
- 3 Ounces Cream Cheese, Fat Free
- 4 Ounces Cream of Chicken Soup, Fat Free

Directions:

1. Place all ingredients into your instant pot, and then set the pressure manually for fifteen minutes.
2. Use a natural pressure release for five minutes before using a quick release.
3. Serve immediately.

Buttermilk & Herb Chicken

Ingredients:

- 1 lb Chicken, Boneless
- ½ Cup Buttermilk
- ½ Teaspoon Sage, Dried
- ½ Teaspoon Black Pepper
- ½ Teaspoon Sea Salt, Fine
- ½ Tablespoon Rosemary, Dried
- ½ Teaspoon Thyme, Dried
- ½ Tablespoon Honey, Raw
- ½ Tablespoon Dijon Mustard

Directions:

1. Place all ingredients together in a bowl and allow to marinate for about one hour.
2. Place the chicken breasts and marinade in your instant pot.
3. Lock and cover the lid, manually setting the pressure for fifteen minutes.
4. Use a natural pressure release for five minutes before using a quick release.
5. Serve warm.

Chicken Parmigiana

Ingredients:

- 1/6 Cup Olive Oil
- ½ lb Chicken, Boneless Breasts
- 1/6 Cup Parmesan Cheese, Grated
- 1/8 Teaspoon Garlic Powder
- ¾-1 Tablespoon Butter, Salted
- 8 Ounces Tomato Sauce
- ¼ Cup Mozzarella Cheese, Shredded

Directions:

1. Heat your oil using the sauté setting for your instant pot.
2. Brown each piece of chicken on each side before adding your garlic powder, butter, and parmesan cheese and tomato sauce.
3. Lock the lid, and then cook using the manual setting for fifteen minutes.
4. Use a quick release.
5. Sprinkle with mozzarella before serving. Alternatively, use the keep warm function and allow the mozzarella to melt before serving.

Cilantro Lime Chicken

Ingredients:

- 1 Tablespoon Olive Oil
- 1 Teaspoon Minced Garlic
- 1/8 Cup Lime Juice
- 1 Tablespoon Cilantro, Fresh & Chopped
- Sea Salt & Pepper to Taste
- 1 lb Chicken Breasts, Quartered & Boneless

Directions:

1. Place your chicken in your instant pot.
2. Mix your lime juice, olive oil, garlic, salt, pepper and cilantro in a bowl before pouring it on top of your chicken.
3. Set on the poultry setting, and then adjust the time to nine minutes.
4. Allow the pressure to release naturally for five minutes before using a quick release.
5. Serve warm.

Apple & Bacon Chicken

Ingredients:

- 4 Ounces Tomato Paste
- 1 ½ Tablespoons Molasses
- ½ Tablespoon Maple syrup
- ½ Tablespoon Apple Cider Vinegar
- 1 Tablespoon Coconut Aminos
- 1 Teaspoon Garlic, Minced
- 1 Teaspoon Smoked Paprika
- ½ Tablespoon Dijon Mustard
- Sea Salt to Taste
- 2/3 Cup Onion, Diced
- 2 Cups Apple, Diced
- 4 Individual Bacon Slices
- 1 lb Chicken Breasts, Boneless & Quartered

Directions:

1. Combine your tomato paste, molasses, apple cider vinegar, coconut aminos, maple syrup, garlic, Dijon mustard, sea salt and smoked paprika together.
2. Stir in your apples and onions.
3. Wrap your bacon slices around your chicken breast, and then place them in the instant pot with your BBQ mix.
4. Lock the lid, and then cook using the manual setting for ten minutes.
5. Use a natural pressure release before using a quick release for the remaining steam.
6. Serve immediately.

Citrus & Herb Chicken

Ingredients:

- 2 Chicken Thighs, Bone In & Large
- 1/8 Cup Lemon Juice
- ¼ Cup Tangerine Juice
- 1/8 Cup White Wine
- 1 Teaspoon Garlic, Minced
- ½ Teaspoon Rosemary, Fresh & Chopped
- ¼ Teaspoon Thyme, Dried
- Sea Salt & Black Pepper to Taste

Directions:

1. Start by placing your chicken thighs in the inner pot.
2. Combine your tangerine juice, lemon juice, garlic, rosemary, wine, and thyme, salt and pepper together. Pour it over the chicken, and then lock your instant pot.
3. Set it on the poultry setting for a half hour.
4. Use a natural pressure release for five minutes before using a quick release for the remaining steam.
5. Serve warm.

Cranberry Beef

Ingredients:

- 1 ¼ lb Beef Roast, Quartered
- ½ Tablespoon Minced Onion, Dried
- 6 Ounces Cranberries, Fresh
- ¼ Cup Orange Juice
- ¼ Cup Water
- ¼ Cup Brown Sugar
- ¼ Cup Sugar
- ¼ Teaspoon Cinnamon

Directions:

1. Combine your cranberries, orange juice, water, white sugar, brown sugar and cinnamon together, mixing well. Place it into your instant pot, and thins sauté for five minutes. Your cranberries should start to burst.
2. Add your dried onions and roast, locking the lid.
3. Cook on manual for thirty to forty minutes depending on how you like your roast done.
4. Release the pressure naturally. It should take about fifteen minutes.
5. Remove the roast and cranberries with a slotted spoon to serve.

Beef with Cheesy Noodles

Ingredients:

- 1 ¼ Cup Ground Beef
- 8 Ounces Tomatoes, Diced & Canned
- ¼ Cup Onions, Diced
- 1/8 Teaspoon Garlic Powder
- 1/2-1 Beef Bouillon Cube
- 2 Tablespoons Water
- ¾ Cup Bell Pepper, Sliced
- 1 Tablespoon Soy Sauce, Low Sodium
- ½ Teaspoon Sugar
- ½ Tablespoon Cornstarch
- 4 Ounces Egg Noodles, Cooked
- 2 Ounces Cheddar Cheese, Shredded

Directions:

1. Combine your tomatoes, beef, onions, beef bouillon, water and garlic powder together.
2. Cook on manual for ten minutes, using a quick pressure release.
3. Add in your sugar, cornstarch, green peppers and soy sauce. Sauté for a few minutes.
4. Cook your noodles according to package directions if they are not already cooked.
5. Combine your cheese and noodles, and serve your instant pot mix over the noodles while still warm.

Umami Pot Roast

Ingredients:

- 1 lb Chuck Roast
- 4 Cloves Garlic, Minced
- 1 Small Onion, Sliced
- 1 Cup Chicken Stock, Unsalted
- 1 Tablespoon Light Soy Sauce
- 1 Tablespoon Fish Sauce
- 1 Tablespoon Olive Oil
- 1 Pinch Dried Rosemary
- 1 Pinch Thyme
- 2 Bay Leaves
- 2 Tablespoons Red Wine
- Sea Salt & Pepper to Taste
- 2 Carrots, Chopped
- 8 White Mushrooms, Sliced
- 3 Potatoes, Quartered
- 1 ½ Tablespoons Cornstarch
- 2 Tablespoons Water

Directions:

1. Pat your roast down with a paper towel before seasoning with salt and pepper.
2. Brown your chuck roast using the sauté button on your instant pot. Add a tablespoon of olive oil into the pot, and then add in your chuck roast. Let it brown for ten minutes on each side. Remove and set it to the side.
3. Sauté your garlic and onion in the instant pot, making sure to slice your onions first.
4. Cook until your onion begins to soften and add the garlic. Cook until fragrant which will take about thirty seconds. Add in your mushrooms and then cook for another two minutes.
5. Pour in your red wine to deglaze your instant pot.
6. Add all other ingredients, and press the manual setting, cooking for forty minutes.

Beef Curry

Ingredients:

- ½ lb Beef Stew Meat, Chunked
- 1 Tablespoon Ghee
- 1 Small Onion, Diced
- 1-2 Potatoes
- 3 Carrots
- 3 Cloves Garlic
- ½ Cup Coconut Milk
- ¼ Cup Bone Broth
- 1 ½ Tablespoons Curry Powder
- ½ Teaspoon Sea Salt
- ¼ Teaspoon Black Pepper
- ½ Teaspoon Oregano, Dried
- ¼ Teaspoon Paprika

Directions:

1. Cut the potatoes, carrots and onion, and then dice the garlic.
2. Press the sauté button, and then put the ghee in your instant pot. Once melted, add your onions and garlic. Cook while stirring for two minutes.
3. Add the stew meat, cooking until it's browned on all sides. This should take roughly five minutes.
4. Turn the instant pot off, and then add in the remaining ingredients. Stir well.
5. Place the lid on, and then cook for thirty minutes using your manual button.
6. Serve warm over rice.

Easy Thai Chicken

Ingredients:

- 1 Inch Ginger, Grated & Minced
- 1 Medium Red Onion, Sliced Thick
- 4 Garlic Cloves, Minced
- 2 Chicken Breasts, Diced
- Lime, Zested & Juiced
- 4 Inch Stem Lemongrass, Ends Removed & Halved
- 15 Mint Leaves
- 2 Tablespoons Butter
- 1 Teaspoon Sea Salt
- ½ Cup Coconut Milk, Full Fat
- ½ Teaspoon Curry Powder
- ½ Cup Chicken Broth
- ¼ Cup Coconut Aminos

Directions:

1. Press sauté on your instant pot, and then add in your button. Add the garlic, onions and ginger, cooking for five minutes while stirring occasionally.
2. Add in your chicken, stirring occasionally for two to three minutes. The pink color should be completely gone.
3. Turn your instant pot off, adding in your lemongrass, lime zest, lime juice, curry powder, mint leaves, bone broth, coconut milk, and coconut aminos. Stir to combine, and then lock the lid.
4. Press your poultry setting, reducing the time to ten minutes.
5. Use a quick release, and then serve immediately. Some people prefer to garnish with lime wedges and cilantro before serving over white rice.

Cajun Chicken Fried Rice

Ingredients:

- ½ lb Chicken Breast
- ½ Tablespoon Cajun Seasoning, Divided
- ½ Tablespoon Olive Oil
- ½ Small Onion, Diced
- 1-2 Cloves Garlic, Minced
- ½ Tablespoon Tomato Paste
- 1 ½ Cups Rice, Rinsed
- ½ Bell Pepper, Chunked
- 1 Cup Chicken Broth

Directions:

1. Start by cutting your chicken breath lengthwise in half, making them thinner. Season with Cajun seasoning on both sides.
2. Heat the instant pot using the sauté button, and then add your oil. Sauté your garlic and onion until it's lightly browned. Turn it off by pressing cancel.
3. Stir in your tomato paste, and then add in your remaining Cajun seasoning, bell peppers and rinsed rice. Stir until combined.
4. Pour your broth into your instant pot, mixing well. Arrange your chicken breast halves on top.
5. Seal the lid and use the manual setting to cook for ten minutes.
6. Release the pressure for a natural pressure release for ten minutes, and then use a quick pressure release for the rest.
7. Shred the chicken and stir to combine.
8. Serve with chopped cilantro while still warm.

Instant Pot Crab

Ingredients:

- 1 lb Crab Legs, Frozen
- 2 Tablespoons Butter, Melted
- 2/3 Cup Water
- Lemon Juice to Taste

Directions:

1. Put your steamer basket in your instant pot, and then place your crab legs in it.
2. Pour the water in and seal the lid.
3. Cook on high pressure for two minutes before using a quick release.
4. Mix your butter and lemon juice together. Serve it as a dipping sauce to your crabs.

Shrimp Biryani

Ingredients:

- ½ Cup Basmati Rice, Soaked in Cold Water (15-30 Minutes)
- 1 Tablespoon Ghee
- ½ Tablespoon Cashews, Raw & Halved
- ½ Tablespoon Golden Raisins
- 1 Red Onion, Sliced
- 1 Teaspoon Garlic, Minced
- 1 Teaspoon Ginger
- ¼ Teaspoon Cumin Seeds
- ½" Cinnamon Stick
- 1 Clove, Whole
- 2 Cardamom Pods
- 10 Curry Leaves
- ½ Green Chili, Minced
- ½ Tomato, Diced
- ¼ Teaspoon Ground Turmeric
- ¼ Teaspoon Black Pepper
- ½ Teaspoon Sea Salt, Fine
- ½ Teaspoon Paprika
- ½ Teaspoon Garam Masala
- 1 Cup Water
- ½ lb Jumbo Shrimp, Raw
- Cilantro to Garnish
- Mint to Garnish

Directions:

1. Soak your basmati rice in cool water for fifteen to thirty minutes. Drain the rice, rinse it and set it to the side.
2. Press sauté on your instant pot, adding in your ghee. Once your ghee has melted, add in your raisins and cashews. Stir fry for about two minutes. The cashews should turn a golden color, and you can remove them. Set them aside for later for garnish.
3. Add in your whole spices and onions, stir frying for ten to twelve minutes. The onions should start to brown.

4. At this pint add in your chili pepper, curry leaves, garlic, and ginger, stirring to combine. Add the tomatoes and ground spices, stir frying for three to four minutes. Your tomato should begin to break down.
5. Add the rice and water, stirring before adding in your shrimp.
6. Secure the lid, cooking on high pressure for six minutes.
7. Use a natural pressure release for ten minutes, and then release the rest of the pressure with a quick pressure release.
8. Garnish with mint, cashews and cilantro.

Jumbo Teriyaki Scallops

Ingredients:

- 1 Tablespoon Avocado Oil
- 1 lb Jumbo Sea Scallops, Fresh
- ½ Cup Coconut Aminos
- 3 Tablespoons Maple Syrup, Pure
- ½ Teaspoon Garlic Powder
- ½ Teaspoon Ginger, Ground
- ½ Teaspoon Sea Salt, Fine
- Minced Chives to Garnish

Directions:

1. Pour your avocado oil into your instant pot and press sauté.
2. Sear your scallops for a minute on each side.
3. Whisk all remaining ingredients except for your chives together while your scallops are searing.
4. Pour the sauce over your scallops, and then press the steam button. Adjust the time to two minutes, and then use a quick release.
5. Serve garnished with chives.

Easy Shrimp

Ingredients:

- 1 lb Shrimp
- 1 Tablespoon Oil
- 1 Tablespoon Butter
- ½ Tablespoon Garlic, Minced
- ¼ Cup Chicken Stock
- ¼ Cup White Wine
- ½ Tablespoon Lemon Juice
- Parsley to Garnish
- ½ Box Pasta, Cooked
- Sea Salt & Black Pepper to Taste

Directions:

1. Place your oil and butter into your instant pot and press sauté. Once your butter is melted add your garlic, cooking until fragrant.
2. Add your chicken stock and white wine, using it to deglaze your pot. Stir up any browned bits.
3. Turn off your sauté, and then add your shrimp. Place the lid on, and then use the stew button. Cook for a minute and use a natural pressure release for five minutes.
4. Stir in your cooked pasta, adding your lemon, salt and pepper to taste.
5. Garnish with parsley before serving.

Herb Scallops & Vegetables

Ingredients:

- 1/3 Cup Chicken Broth
- 1 Tablespoon Extra Virgin Olive Oil
- 1 Tablespoon Lemon Juice
- 1 Pinch Sea Salt, Fine
- ¼ Teaspoon Basil, Dried
- ¼ Teaspoon Onion Powder
- ¼ Teaspoon Garlic, Minced
- 6 Ounces Scallops
- 1 Cup Kale, Chopped
- 2 Tablespoons Greek Salad Dressing

Directions:

1. Place your broth and salt into your pot, and then put the steamer on top. Toss your scallops in the dressing before adding your seasoning. Place the scallops and vegetables on top of your steamer.
2. Cook for three minutes using your steam button, and then use a quick release.
3. Remove the basket and then drain the water.
4. Cook on sauté until seared before serving.

Shrimp & Asparagus

Ingredients:

- 1 lb Shrimp, Fresh, Peeled & Deveined
- 1 Bunch Asparagus
- ½ Tablespoon Cajun Seasoning
- 1 Teaspoon Olive Oil

Directions:

1. Add a cup of water to your instant pot, and then insert the steamer basket into your instant pot.
2. Place your asparagus on the steam rack in a single layer. Add your shrimp on top.
3. Drizzle your Cajun seasoning and olive oil over it.
4. Cover and lock the lid. Use the steam mode, adjusting the time to two minutes. Select low pressure, and then use a quick release.
5. Serve warm.

Ginger Scallion Fish

Ingredients:

Fish & Sauce:

- 1 ½ Tablespoons Soy Sauce
- 1 Tablespoon Rice Wine
- ½ Tablespoon Chinese Black Bean Paste
- ½ Teaspoon Garlic, Minced
- ½ Teaspoon Ginger, Minced
- 1 lb Firm White Fish (Such as Tilapia)

Vegetables:

- ½ Tablespoon Peanut Oil
- 1 Tablespoon Ginger, Julienned
- 1/8 Cup Green Scallions, Sliced Thin
- 1/8 Cup Cilantro, Fresh & Chopped

Directions:

1. Put your fish on a plate, and then pour all ingredients for your sauce over it. Let it marinate for twenty to thirty minutes.
2. Chop your vegetables, placing them to the side.
3. Place two cups of water to your instant pot, and then put your steamer in.
4. Remove the fish from the marinade, placing it on the steamer basket. Reserve the marinade for later.
5. Cook on low pressure for two minutes before using a quick release.
6. Drain your water, removing the steamer basket.
7. Sauté your oil in your instant pot before adding in your ginger and scallions. Cook until it's softened, and then add the reserved marinade. Let boil vigorously until cooked through, and then pour over your fish to serve.

Coconut Fish Curry

Ingredients:

- 1 ½ lbs White Fish Fillet, Rinsed & Chopped
- 1 Cup Cherry Tomatoes, Heaping
- 1 Medium Onion, Sliced
- 1 Green Chili, Sliced
- 1 Clove Garlic, Chopped Fine
- ½ Tablespoon Ginger, Grated Fresh
- 3 Curry Leaves
- ½ Tablespoon Ground Coriander
- ½ Tablespoon Ground Cumin
- ¼ Teaspoon Ground Turmeric
- ½ Teaspoon Chili Powder
- ¼ Teaspoon Ground Fenugreek
- 1 Cup Coconut Milk
- Lemon Juice to Taste
- Sea Salt to Taste

Directions:

1. Press the sauté button on your instant pot, adding in your curry leaves and oil. Lightly fry your leaves until they turn golden around the edges. This should take about a minute.
2. Add your ginger, onion and garlic, sautéing until your onion has softened.
3. Add all of your ground spices together, sautéing until they've become aromatic.
4. Deglaze the pot with coconut milk, scraping everything up from the bottom.
5. Add your fish, tomatoes, and green chilies. Stir to coat, and then lock the lid. Cook for three minutes on high pressure before using a quick release.
6. Add your salt and lemon juice before serving.

Mango Chicken Curry

Ingredients:

- 1 Tablespoon Ghee
- 1 ½ Teaspoons Garlic
- ½ Onion, Diced
- 2 Teaspoons Ginger
- 1 ½ Tablespoons Tomato Paste
- 1 Teaspoon Sea Salt, Fine
- 1 Teaspoon Curry Powder
- 1 Teaspoon Cumin
- ½ Teaspoon Turmeric
- ¼ Teaspoon Cayenne
- ¼ Teaspoon Paprika
- 1 ½ lbs Chicken Thighs, Boneless & skinless
- 4 Cups Cauliflower
- 1 Sweet Potato, Diced
- ½ Cup Chicken Stock
- 400 ml Coconut Milk, Canned
- 1 Cup Frozen Mango Pieces
- 1 ½ Cups Baby Spinach
- ½ Lime, Juiced
- ¼ Cup Cilantro, Chopped

Directions:

1. Turn your instant pot to sauté, and then add in your garlic, tomato paste, ghee, onion, curry powder, cumin, salt, turmeric, cayenne, and paprika. Sauté for three minutes. Your spices should become fragrant, and your onions should soften
2. Add in your sweet potato, cauliflower and chicken thighs, stirring to coat liberally with spices.
3. Add in your chicken stock and coconut milk, stirring once more.
4. Turn the statue function off, and then close the lid. Set on high pressure for twenty minutes.
5. Use quick release, and then add in your baby spinach, lime juice and frozen mango.

6. Let it sit for ten minutes before serving topped with cilantro over rice.

Pork Roast with Apple Gravy

Ingredients:

- 2 ½ lbs Pork Shoulder Roast, Bone In
- ½ Teaspoon Sea Salt, Fine
- ¼ Teaspoon Black Pepper
- ½ Tablespoon Olive Oil
- ½ Yellow Onion, Sliced
- 1 Apple, Cored & Sliced
- ½ Cup Chicken Broth
- ½ Cup Apple Juice
- 1 Sprig Rosemary, Fresh
- 2 Sage Leaves, Fresh
- 1 Bay Leaf
- 1 ½ Tablespoons Flour
- 1 ½ Tablespoons Butter

Directions:

1. Rinse and pat your roast dry, seasoning with salt and pepper.
2. Heat your instant pot using the sauté function. Add your pork roast, browning for five minutes on both sides.
3. Add in your apples, broth, juice, onion, sage, rosemary and bay leaf. Close the lid, setting to high pressure. Cook for a full hour, and then allow for a natural pressure release.
4. Carefully remove your roast before tenting it with aluminum foil.
5. Strain out solids from the liquid, and then discard the solids. Save the liquid for your gravy.
6. Place your instant pot on sauté again, and heat our flour and butter, cooking until golden brown while stirring. This should take three to five minutes. Whisk while hot to form the gravy.
7. Plate your pork, drizzling gravy over top of it to serve.

Wild Alaskan Cod

Ingredients:

- 2 Filets Wild Alaskan Cod
- 2 Cups Cherry Tomatoes
- 4 Tablespoons Butter
- Sea Salt & Black Pepper to Taste

Directions:

1. Take an oven safe dish that fits in your instant pot, putting your tomatoes in it.
2. Cut your fillets before laying it on top of the tomatoes.
3. Season with salt and pepper.
4. Pat with butter, and then drizzle some olive oil over it.
5. Pour in a cup of water into your instant pot and then put the trivet inside.
6. Place the oven safe dish on the trivet, locking the lid.
7. Use high pressure, cooking for five minutes.
8. Use a quick release, and then serve.

Fish Chowder

Ingredients:

- 1/3 Cup Bacon, Chopped
- ½ Onion, Chopped
- 1 Ribs Celery, Chopped
- 1 Small Carrot, Chopped
- 1 Clove Garlic, Minced
- 1 ½ Cups Potatoes, Cubed & Peeled
- 2 Cups Chicken Bone Broth
- 1 Tablespoon Butter
- ½ lb Haddock Fillets, Frozen
- ½ Cup Corn, Frozen
- 1 Cup Heavy Cream
- ½ Tablespoon Potato Starch
- Sea Salt & White Pepper to Taste

Directions:

1. Press sauté on your instant pot, adding in your butter and bacon. Cook until your bacon is crispy.
2. Add in your carrot, onion, garlic and celery. Cook for about three minutes. Your vegetables should become soft, and then season with salt and pepper.
3. Add in your potatoes, fish, broth and corn. Cook on high pressure for five minutes.
4. Allow for a natural pressure release, and then combine your heavy cream and potato starch. Mix well.
5. Add this to your chowder, mixing well. Press the warm button, and allow for it to thicken for two to three minutes before serving.

Vietnamese Caramel Salmon

Ingredients:

- ½ Tablespoon Coconut Oil
- 1/6 Cup Light Brown Sugar
- 1 ½ Tablespoons Asian Fish Sauce
- ¾ Tablespoon Soy Sauce
- ½ Teaspoon Ginger, Peeled & Grated
- Zest of 1 Small Lime
- ¼ Lime, Juiced
- ¼ Teaspoon Ground Black Pepper
- 2 Skinless Salmon Fillets, 6-8 Ounces
- Scallions, Sliced for Garnish
- Cilantro Leaves for Garnish

Directions:

1. Use the sauté function, whisking together your brown sugar, fish sauce, oil, soy sauce, lime zest, lime juice, black pepper and ginger. Bring it to a simmer, and then turn off the heat.
2. Place your fish in your pressure cooker with the skin side up.
3. Spoon the sauce over your fish, covering and cooking on low pressure for one minute. Use a natural pressure release for five minutes, and then use a quick release for the remaining pressure. If you want it to cook a little more, use your sauté button and cook for another minute.
4. Flip your salmon over as you place them on a serving platter. Press sauté on your instant pot, and cook for about three minutes. This should become thick and syrupy.
5. Spoon it over your salmon before serving, and garnish with cilantro and scallions.

Country Ribs

Ingredients:

- 1 ½ lbs Country Style Pork Ribs
- ½ Tablespoon Brown Sugar
- ½ Teaspoon Salt
- ½ Teaspoon Paprika
- ½ Teaspoon Garlic
- ½ Teaspoon Onion Powder
- ½ Teaspoon Black Pepper
- ½ Teaspoon Cumin
- ¼ Teaspoon Cayenne Pepper
- 1/3 Cup Beef Broth
- ¼ Cup BBQ Sauce + Some for Serving

Directions:

1. Take a small bowl, mixing all dry rub ingredients together.
2. Spread the dry rub on the ribs and massage it into the meat.
3. Pour the beef broth into your instant pot, adding your ribs on top. Pour the BBQ sauce, and lock the lid on the pressure cooker.
4. Cook on high pressure for forty-five minutes. Use a natural pressure release.
5. Remove ribs, and serve warm. Add more BBQ sauce if desired.

Char Siu

Ingredients:

Pork:

- 1 lb Pork Butt Meat, Split in Half
- 3 Tablespoons Honey, raw
- 2 Tablespoons Light Soy Sauce
- 1 Cup Water
- Sea Salt to Taste

Marinade:

- 1 Tablespoon Chu Hou Paste
- 2 Cubes Chinese Fermented Red Bean Curd
- 3 Tablespoons Char Siu Sauce
- ½ Tablespoon Sesame Oil
- 2 Tablespoons Shaoxing Wine
- 1 Teaspoon Garlic Powder
- 1 Tablespoon Light Soy Sauce

Directions:

1. Start by marinating your pork. Poke holes all over it, and then mix all marinade ingredients together. Marinate for a half hour to two hours.
2. Remove the pork from the bag before adding a cup of water to the bag to get out the remaining marinade.
3. Pour the remaining mixture into your instant pot, and place your pork butt meat in the steamer basket. Season with salt, and cook on high pressure for eighteen minutes. Use a natural pressure release, which will take about twelve minutes.
4. Mix two tablespoons of soy sauce with your honey in a bowl, and then brush it over the pork butt meat.
5. Preheat your oven to 450, and then cook your pork butt in it for four to six minutes. It should brown.
6. Serve with rice or noodles. Many people pout the leftover honey sauce on the side.

Short Rib Soup

Ingredients:

- 2 Green Onions, For Cooking Broth
- 2 Green Onions, Sliced for Garnish
- 1 Yellow Onion
- 8 Cups Water
- 1 ½ lbs Beef Short Ribs
- 2 Slices Ginger, Thick
- ½ Korean Radish, Cut into Chunks
- 2 Tablespoons Garlic, Chopped
- 2 Teaspoons Guk Ganjang (Korean Soy Sauce for Soup)
- 1 Teaspoon Korean Chonilyeom Sea Salt (Less if using Table Salt)

Directions:

1. Trim the excess fat from the ribs, and then soak the ribs in cold water for a half hour. This will draw out excess blood.
2. While soaking the ribs, clean your green onions, slicing two of them. Cut the remaining two for soup.
3. Peel and cut the ginger before chopping your radishes. If you do not have a Korean radish, a good substitute is a Daikon radish. Peel the onion, and then place everything except for your sliced green onion, salt, garlic and guk ganjang in your instant pot.
4. Click the soup function, and then cook for a half hour.
5. Use a quick release for the pressure, and skim the excess fat out. Oil absorbing paper is a great way to do this.
6. Season the soup with your guk ganjang, salt and garlic.
7. Serve garnished with your green onions.

Orange Chicken

Ingredients:

- 2 Chicken Breasts, Thick Breasts
- 1/3 Cup Sweet Barbeque Sauce
- 1 Tablespoon Soy Sauce
- ½ Teaspoon Cornstarch
- Green Onions, Sliced for Garnish
- 1/3 Cup Orange Marmalade

Directions:

1. Chop your chicken breasts into bite size chunks. Add your chicken, soy sauce and barbeque sauce to your instant pot.
2. Cook on high pressure for four minutes.
3. Use a quick release when done. Take 1/8 cup barbeque sauce out of your sauce, and then mix your cornstarch in.
4. Add your cornstarch back into your broth mixture.
5. Add in your orange marmalade, mixing well.
6. Change the setting to sauté, cooking for six minutes.
7. Allow it to rest for five minutes before serving. The sauce should thicken.
8. Garnish with green onions before serving over rice or noodles.

Portuguese Chicken & Rice

Ingredients:

Chicken:

- 3 Chicken Quartered, Cut into 1 Inch Pieces & Deboned
- 1 Medium Carrot, Chunked
- 1 Small Onion, Sliced
- 3 Cloves Garlic, Minced
- 1 Small Shallot, Sliced
- 1 Green Bell Pepper, Cubed
- 2 Small Bay Leaves
- ¾ Cup Coconut Milk
- 1 Tablespoon Soy Sauce
- Tablespoon Peanut Oil
- 1 ½ Teaspoons Turmeric Powder
- 1 Teaspoon Ground Cumin
- 1 ½ Tablespoons Cornstarch + 2 Tablespoons Water (Mixed)
- Sea Salt & Black Pepper to Taste

Marinade:

- 1 Tablespoon Shaoxiing Wine
- 1 Tablespoon Light Soy Sauce
- Dash White Pepper
- ½ Teaspoon White Sugar

Rice:

- Just under 1 Cup Water
- 1 Cup + 1 ½ Tablespoons Jasmine Rice

Directions:

1. Mix your marinade together, and then marinate your chicken thighs.
2. Prepare your pressure cooker by pressing the sauté button. Add in your onions, peanut oil, garlic and shallot, cooking until your

onions are browned and it's fragrant. Season with salt and pepper if desired.

3. Pour in your chicken, sauté until browned. Add in your turmeric and cumin before sautéing well. Mix with spices, adding your carrots, bay leave sand potatoes. Mix thoroughly.
4. Deglaze with a tablespoon of soy sauce and your coconut milk.
5. Place a steamer rack into the pressure cooker, and place a bowl with your jasmine rice on the rack.
6. Pour in your water, and then close the lid. Cook on high pressure for four minutes. Allow for a natural pressure release.

Pork Chops with Onion Sauce

Ingredients:

- 2 Boneless Pork Loin Chops, 1 ¼ Inches Thick
- 1 Small Onion, Sliced
- ½ Tablespoon Olive Oil
- ½ Tablespoon Balsamic Vinegar
- ½ Tablespoon Worcestershire Sauce
- ½ Tablespoon Light Soy Sauce
- ½ Teaspoon Sugar
- ½ Cup Chicken Stock
- ¾ Tablespoons Cornstarch + 2 Tablespoons Water, Mixed
- Sea Salt to Taste

Marinade:

- ½ Tablespoon Light Soy Sauce
- ¼ Teaspoon Sea Salt
- ½ Tablespoon Shaoxing Wine
- ¼ Teaspoon Sugar
- ¼ Teaspoon White Pepper
- ¼ Teaspoon Sesame Oil

Directions:

1. Pound your pork chops to make sure that they're tender.
2. Mix all ingredients for your marinade together, and then place your pork chops inside. Marinate for twenty minutes.
3. Prepare your pressure cooker by pressing sauté. Add in your pork chops, adding in your oil. Brown for one to one and a half minutes on each side, and make sure they don't burn. Remove from your instant pot, and set it to the side.
4. Add in your onions, salt and pepper together. Cook your onions for about a minute or until softened.
5. Use your balsamic vinegar to partially deglaze your pot.
6. Add your chicken stock, Worcestershire, light soy sauce, and sugar together. Mix well, and fully deglaze your pot.

7. Place your pork chops with the meat juices in your pot, cooking on high pressure for one minute.
8. Allow for a natural pressure release, which will take about ten minutes.
9. Remove your pork chops, setting it to the side. Mix your cornstarch and water together, placing it into the sauce. Cook on sauté until it's thickened as desired.

Middle Eastern Lamb Stew

Ingredients:

- ½ Onion, Diced
- ¾-1 lb Lamb Stew Meat
- 1 Tablespoon Olive Oil
- 3-4 Garlic Cloves, Roughly Chopped
- ½ Teaspoon Sea Salt
- ½ Teaspoon Pepper
- ½ Teaspoon Cumin
- ½ Teaspoon Turmeric
- ½ Teaspoon Coriander
- ½ Teaspoon Cumin Seeds
- ½ Teaspoon Cinnamon
- Tablespoon tomato Paste
- 1/8 Cup Apple Cider Vinegar
- ¼ Teaspoon Chili Flakes
- 1 Tablespoon Honey, Raw
- ¾ Cup Chicken Stock
- 8 Ounces Chickpeas, Rinsed & Drained
- 1/8 Cup Raisins

Directions:

1. Turn on your instant pot before hitting the sauté function. Heat your oil and onions together. Cooking until fragrant.
2. Add your garlic, lamb, spices and salt together. Cook for another five minutes.
3. Add in your tomato paste, vinegar, honey, stock, raisins, and chickpeas. Stir until combined.
4. Cover, and then click meat stew, cooking for an hour. If you don't have that setting just cook on high pressure.
5. Use a quick release, and then stir.
6. Serve over rice or quinoa.

Side Dishes

Many of the recipes in the previous chapter are one pot meals, but some do require side dishes. Here are a few easy side dishes you can make in your instant pot to put easy dinners on the table.

Bhindi Masala

Ingredients:

- 1 lb Okra or Bhindi, Cut into 1 Inch Pieces
- 1 Onion, Sliced
- 1 Tomato, Chopped
- 1 Tablespoon Olive Oil
- ½ Teaspoon Cumin Seeds
- 3 Pods Garlic
- ¼ Teaspoons Turmeric
- 1 Teaspoon Coriander
- ¼ Teaspoon Cayenne Powder
- 1 Teaspoon Aamchur Powder
- 1 Teaspoon Sea Salt, Fine

Directions:

1. Heat your instant pot using the sauté function, adding your oil, garlic and cumin. Sauté for thirty seconds.
2. Add your sliced onion, sautéing for another three minutes.
3. Add in your spices, okra and tomato. Mix well, and then use the manual function to cook at low pressure for two minutes.
4. Use a quick release, and then stir the okra in gently. Allow to cool for five minutes before serving.

Vinegar & Maple Braised Parsnips

Ingredients:

- 1 ½ lbs Parsnips, Peeled & Cut into ½ Inch Slices
- ¼ Cup Vegetable Broth
- 3 Tablespoons Balsamic Vinegar
- 2 Tablespoons Maple Syrup
- ½ Teaspoon Sea Salt, Fine
- Ground Black Pepper to Taste

Directions:

1. Add your vegetable broth, vinegar and parsnips to your instant pot.
2. Bring it to high pressure, cooking for three minutes.
3. Use a quick release, and then add your balsamic vinegar and maple before serving. Make sure to stir to coat.

Cajun Zucchini

Ingredients:

- 2 Zucchinis, Sliced
- ½ Tablespoon Butter
- ½ Cup Water
- 1 Tablespoon Cajun Seasoning
- ½ Teaspoon Paprika
- ½ Teaspoon Garlic Powder

Directions:

1. Place all ingredient into your instant pot, stirring.
2. Set on low pressure for one minute.
3. Serve as a side dish while still warm.

Parmesan Zoodles

Ingredients:

- 2 Tablespoons Olive Oil
- 1 Tablespoon Mint, Sliced Thin
- 4 Tablespoons Parmesan, Grated
- 1/3 Lemon, Juiced
- 2 Large Zucchinis, Spiralized
- ½ Lemon, zested
- ½ Teaspoon Sea Salt, Fine
- 2 Cloves Garlic, Finely Diced
- Black Pepper to taste

Directions:

1. Prepare all ingredients before you start.
2. Press the sauté on your instant pot, and then add in your garlic, olive oil, lemon zest and salt, stirring. Cook for thirty seconds or until it becomes fragrant and golden brown.
3. Add the zucchini noodles, drizzled with lemon juice.
4. Stir through, adding your garlic and lemon zest. Do not actually cook your noodles. Just heat them up.
5. Sprinkle with mint and parmesan, stirring through and serving right away.

Kale & Carrots

Ingredients:

- 10 Ounces Kale, Chopped Roughly
- 1 Tablespoon Ghee
- 1 Onion, Sliced Thin
- 3 Carrots, Cut into ½ Inch Pieces
- 5 Cloves Garlic, Peeled & Chopped Roughly
- ½ Cup chicken Broth
- Aged Balsamic Vinegar
- ¼ Teaspoon Red Pepper Flakes
- Sea Salt & Black Pepper

Directions:

1. Press the sauté button, and then toss in your onion and carrots. Sauté until they've softened.
2. Throw in the garlic, cooking for about thirty seconds or until fragrant. Pile in your kale, and then pour in your broth. Sprinkle it with salt and pepper, and then lock the lid in place.
3. Cook on high pressure for five minutes.
4. Allow for a natural pressure release, and then add balsamic vinegar to taste.
5. Sprinkle with red pepper flakes before serving.

Bell Pepper & Potatoes

Ingredients:

- 1 Tablespoon Olive Oil
- 2 Bell Peppers, Sliced
- 4 Baby Potatoes, Chopped Small
- ½ Teaspoon Cumin Seeds
- 4 Cloves Garlic, Minced
- ½ Teaspoon Dry Mango Powder (or ½ Tablespoon Lemon Juice)
- Cilantro to Garnish
- 1 Teaspoon Sea Salt, Fine
- 2 Teaspoons Coriander Powder
- ½ Teaspoon Cayenne Powder
- ¼ Teaspoon Turmeric

Directions:

1. Heat your pot using sauté, and then add your garlic, cumin and oil.
2. Once your garlic turns a golden brown, add in your spices, bell pepper and potatoes. Mix well.
3. Change it to manual mode, cooking on high pressure for two minutes. Use a quick release.
4. Stir in your dry mango powder or lemon juice, and serve garnished with cilantro.

Mashed Turnips

Ingredients:

- 2 Turnips, Peeled & Diced
- ½ Small Onion, Peeled & Diced
- ½-1 Cup Beef Broth
- 1/8 Cup Sour Cream
- Sea Salt & Black Pepper to Taste

Directions:

1. Add your onion, broth and turnips to your instant pot. Lock the lid, and bring it to high pressure. Cook for five minutes.
2. Allow for a natural pressure release, and then drain the turnips into a bowl.
3. Use a hand mixer to mash them. Add some of the broth if necessary to thin them, and then stir in your sour cream. Add your sea salt and pepper to taste.

Spanish Potatoes

Ingredients:

- 1 ½ lbs Red Potatoes, Small
- 1 Teaspoon Sea Salt, Fine
- 1 Tablespoon Water
- 1 Teaspoon Tomato Paste
- ½ Tablespoon Brown Rice Flour
- 1 Teaspoon Smoked Spanish Paprika
- ½ Teaspoon Garlic Powder
- 1 Teaspoon Hot Smoked Paprika
- ½ Teaspoon Sea Salt

Directions:

1. Wash your potatoes, and then cut the small ones in half. If they're medium then you need to quarter the. They should be 1 ½ inches at the widest point.
2. Place your potatoes in your instant pot with a cup of water, and ten add a teaspoon of salt. Seal, cooking with high pressure for four minutes.
3. Use a quick pressure release once done.
4. Drain your potatoes, and then put them in a large bowl.
5. Combine your water and tomato paste in another bowl, and then mix your flour with all remaining ingredients.
6. Add your tomato paste mixture to your potatoes, and then gently coat your potatoes. Sprinkle the dry seasoning on your potatoes, and then stir to coat.
7. Drain your instant pot, and then press sauté. Add in your potatoes and lightly brown before serving.

Spicy & Sweet Cabbage

Ingredients:

- ½ Tablespoon Sesame Oil
- 1 Small Carrot, Grated
- ½ Medium Cabbage, Divided into 4 Wedges
- ¾ Cups + 2 Teaspoons Water, Divided
- 1/8 Cup Apple Cider Vinegar
- ½ Teaspoon Demerara Sugar, Raw
- ¼ Teaspoon Cayenne Powder
- ¼ Teaspoon Red Pepper Flakes
- 1 Teaspoon Cornstarch

Directions:

1. Start by putting your instant pot on sauté, adding in your sesame oil. Brown your cabbage wedges on both sides. This should take about three minutes.
2. Add your water, vinegar, cayenne, sugar and hot pepper flakes with your cabbage, sprinkling your carrots on top.
3. Close the lid, and cook at high pressure for five minutes. Use a natural pressure release, and then take the cabbage out.
4. Press sauté again, and bring your cooking liquid to a boil. Mix your teaspoon of water and cornstarch together, making a slurry.
5. Place this into your pressure cooker, cooking until thickened.

Achari Aloo

Ingredients:

- /2 Tablespoon Cumin Seeds
- ½ Tablespoon Coriander Seeds, Pounded
- 3 Cloves
- 1 Bay Leaf
- ½ Teaspoon Sea Salt, Fine
- ¼ Teaspoon Red Chili Powder
- ¼ Teaspoon Turmeric Powder
- ½ Teaspoon Dry Pomegranate Powder
- 1 Teaspoon Fenugreek Leaves, Dried
- ½ Tablespoon Mango Pickle
- 1 Tablespoon + 1 Tablespoon Oil
- 3 Potatoes, Boiled & Cubed

Directions:

1. Press the sauté button on your instant pot, adding in a tablespoon of oil. Add in all of your whole spices, letting them simmer. Then add in your dry spices, mixing well.
2. Add the remaining tablespoon of oil and pickle, mix well.
3. Add in your potatoes, coating them well with the spice mixture.
4. Cancel the sauté mode and close the lid.
5. Select manual and set it for two minutes.
6. Serve warm.

Easy Beets

Ingredients:

- 1 Large Beet
- 1 Cup Cold Water

Directions:

1. Rub and wash our beets using cold water. Trim off the greens and stems if needed.
2. Discard and trim the roots.
3. Pour your water into your instant pot, and then place a steamer basket in it.
4. Place your beet in your instant pot cooking on high pressure for twenty-eight minutes. Use a quick release once it's done.

Easy Artichokes

Ingredients:

- 2 Artichokes (about ½ lb)
- 2 Tablespoons Butter, Unsalted
- 4 Cloves Garlic, Minced
- 1 Lemon, Juiced
- Sea Salt to Taste

Directions:

1. Start by submerging your artichokes for five minutes in cold water.
2. Cut the step off and trim an inch from the top of each one.
3. Place a cup of water in your instant pot before placing in a steamer rack. Place your artichokes inside, squeezing the lemon juice on top.
4. Close your instant pot, cooking for nine minutes before using a quick release.
5. While your artichokes are cooking you can now make your garlic butter. Take a small saucepan, heating it over medium low heat. Melt your butter and add in your garlic. Sauté until your garlic turns a golden color. Be careful not to let it burn, and then season with sea salt as it cools.
6. Serve your artichokes drizzled in your garlic butter.

Easy Corn

Ingredients:

- 2 Ears Corn
- 1 Tablespoon Lime Juice
- Sea Salt to Taste
- ½ Teaspoon Chili Powder

Directions:

1. Pour a cup of water into your instant pot. Add in your trivet, placing two ears of corn on each one. Make sure your corn is shucked, and then season.
2. Close the lid, cooking on high pressure for one to two minutes.
3. Use a quick release, and serve with butter while still warm.

Spaghetti Squash

Ingredients:

- 1 Spaghetti Squash, Whole
- 1 Cup Cold Water

Directions:

1. Use a sharp knife to cut your spaghetti squash in half lengthwise.
2. Scoop the seeds out, scraping them out with a spoon.
3. Place a cup of cold water into your pressure cooker before putting your trivet in your instant pot.
4. Place your spaghetti sauce on the trivet, and then cook on high pressure for six minutes.
5. Use a quick release before serving.

Easy Broccoli

Ingredients:

- 1 Head Broccoli, Cut Into Florets
- ½ Cup Water
- 6 Garlic Cloves, Minced
- 1 Tablespoon Peanut Oil
- 1 Tablespoon Chinese Rice Wine
- Sea Salt to Taste

Directions:

1. Pour in your water. Place your steamer rack into your instant pot, adding your florets on top. Lock the pressure cooker, pressing the time for zero minutes. Turn off the heat, add then do a quick release. Open the lid carefully, and then remove the insert to stop the broccoli from cooking.
2. Press sauté, placing all ingredients into your instant pot. Statue until it reaches your desired level of doneness.

Egg Brule

Ingredients:

- 2 Large Eggs
- 1 Cup Cold Water
- 2 Teaspoons Sugar
- Sea Salt to taste

Directions:

1. Start by placing a cup of water into your instant pot before adding your trivet. Put your eggs on top, and then close the lid. Cook on low pressure for five minutes before using a quick release.
2. Peel your soft boiled eggs after running them under cold water.
3. Cut your eggs in half, and then add in a half a teaspoon of sugar and a little salt to each egg. Use a culinary torch to melt the sugar.
4. Serve immediately.

Easy Sweet Potatoes

Ingredients:

- 2 Sweet Potatoes, Whole
- 1 cup Cold Water
- Butter or Maple Syrup for Topping

Directions:

1. Start by rinsing and scrubbing your sweet potatoes using cold water.
2. Place a cup of cold water in your instant pot before placing your steamer rack in it. If your potato is six inches, cook for twenty minutes. If it's eight inches long, cook for thirty minutes. If its ten inches long cook for forty minutes.
3. Do a natural pressure release, which will take roughly ten minutes.
4. Serve with either butter or drizzled with maple syrup.

Mashed Sweet Potatoes

Ingredients:

- 1-2 lbs Sweet Potatoes
- 2 Tablespoons Butter, Unsalted
- ¼ Teaspoon Nutmeg
- 1-2 tablespoons Maple Syrup, Pure
- 1 Cup Cold Water
- Sea Salt to Taste

Directions:

1. Peel and cut your potatoes. It's best to cut it into one inch pieces.
2. Pour a cup of cold water into your instant pot before adding in your steamer basket. Place your potato chunks in the basket, and then cook on high pressure for eight minutes. Turn off heat and use a quick release once done.
3. Place in a large bowl, and partially mash your potatoes before adding all other ingredients.
4. Add sea salt to taste before serving.

Cauliflower Rice

Ingredients:

- 1/4 Teaspoon Parsley, Dried
- ½ Head Cauliflower
- 1 Tablespoon Olive Oil
- 1/8 Teaspoon Sea Salt, Fine
- ¼ Teaspoon Paprika
- 1/8 Teaspoon Turmeric
- 1/8 Teaspoon Cumin
- Lime Wedges
- Fresh Cilantro

Directions:

1. Start by washing your cauliflower, trimming off the leaves.
2. Cut into pieces before putting it into your steam basket in your instant pot. Pour a cup of water under the steamer basket.
3. Close and lock your lid, cooking for one minutes. Use a quick release, and then remove the cauliflower to plate.
4. Pour out the water from your instant pot, and then press the sauté button.
5. Add in your oil and cooked cauliflower.
6. Break up your cauliflower with a potato masher, and then add in all other ingredients.
7. Serve warm.

Broccoli & Cheddar Pasta

Ingredients:

- 1 Cup Milk
- 16 Ounces Cheddar Cheese
- 4 Cups Water
- 1 Cup Broccoli, Frozen
- 1 lb Pasta

Directions:

1. Place your four cups of water in your instant pot.
2. Place your broccoli in your steamer basket on top of your pasta.
3. Place the pot on high pressure, cooking for four minutes. Use a quick release.
4. Remove the water, and then place your pot on sauté. Add in your cheese and milk, stirring until your cheese is melted.
5. Serve warm.

Garlic & Butter Potatoes

Ingredients:

- 500 Grams Potatoes
- 3 Tablespoons Coconut Butter
- 3 Teaspoons Garlic Puree
- Handful Fresh Rosemary & Thyme
- Sea Salt & Pepper to Taste

Directions:

1. Place a cup of water at the bottom of your instant pot, and then place your potatoes in the steamer basket. Add in your herbs and garlic. Season with salt and pepper.
2. Place the lid on the instant pot, and then steam for four minutes.
3. Allow for a natural pressure release and drain the excess butter from the potatoes.
4. Serve topped with fresh herbs.

Cheese & Bacon Asparagus

Ingredients:

- 4 Slices Bacon
- Sea Salt & Pepper to Taste
- 8-9 Ounces Asparagus
- 2 Ounces Soft Cheese

Directions:

1. Place a cup of water at the bottom of your instant pot.
2. Chop the bottom off of your asparagus, and then smother in soft cheese. Wrap your asparagus in bacon. Place them on the steamer rack inside your instant pot.
3. Place the lid on, sealing and steaming for three minutes.
4. Allow it to cool down before serving.

Balsamic Mushrooms

Ingredients:

- ½ lb Mushrooms, Sliced
- 1 ½ Tablespoons Balsamic Vinegar
- 2 Garlic Cloves, Minced
- 1/6 Cup Extra Virgin Olive Oil

Directions:

1. Pour your olive oil into your instant pot and press the sauté button.
2. Add in your mushrooms and garlic cloves, stirring to coast. Sauté for two to three minutes.
3. Turn your instant pot off once your mushrooms have softened.
4. Pour in your balsamic vinegar before sautéing another one to two minutes.

Easy Green Beans

Ingredients:

- ½ lb Green Beans
- 1/8 Cup Bacon Bits
- ¼ Tablespoon Butter
- Sea Salt & Pepper to Taste

Directions:

1. Cut the ends off of your green beans, washing them well.
2. Place a cup of water at the bottom of your instant pot.
3. Place your steamer rack in, and then place your bacon and green beans in the steamer rack. Let them steam for three to five minutes depending on how soft you want them.
4. Place them in a bowl, adding butter. Mix until it's melted, and serve warm.

Easy Collard Greens

Ingredients:

- 1 lb Collard Greens, Shredded
- 3 Cups Chicken Broth
- ¼ Teaspoon Red Pepper Flakes
- Sea Salt & Black Pepper to Taste

Directions:

1. Add all ingredients into your instant to, and then set the time for sixty minutes.
2. After cooking use a quick pressure release.
3. Mix well and enjoy while warm.

Easy Brussel Sprouts

Ingredients:

- 1 Tablespoon Coconut Oil
- ¼ Cup Onion, Chopped
- 1 Teaspoon Garlic, Minced
- 1-2 Strips Bacon, Chopped
- ½ lb Brussel Sprouts, Trimmed but Whole
- ¼ Cup Water
- Sea Salt & Pepper to Taste
- Butter to Taste

Directions:

1. Turn your instant pot to salute, adding in your coconut oil.
2. Add in your onions and garlic next, sautéing for a full minute before adding your bacon.
3. Continue to sauté until your bacon is crisp and your onions are translucent.
4. Add you're Brussels sprouts and a cup of water, seasoning with salt and pepper to taste. Make sure it's stirred to combine, and then cook on low pressure for three minutes.
5. Use a quick release, and then drop in butter, stirring well.
6. Drain the liquid, and serve warm.

Coconut Cabbage

Ingredients:

- ½ Tablespoon Coconut Oil
- ½ Brown Onion, Sliced
- ¾ Teaspoon Sea Salt
- 1 Large Clove Garlic, Diced
- ½ Long Red Chili, Sliced
- ½ Tablespoon Yellow Mustard Seeds
- ½ Tablespoons Curry Powder, Mild
- ½ Tablespoon Turmeric Powder
- ½ Medium Cabbage, Shredded
- 1 Small Carrot, Peeled & Sliced
- 1 Tablespoon Lime Juice
- ¼ Cup Coconut, Unsweetened
- ½ Tablespoon Olive Oil
- 1/3 Cup Water

Directions:

1. Turn your instant pot to sauté, and then add your coconut oil and onion. Salt and then cook for three to four minutes or until softened.
2. Add your garlic, spics and chili, cooking for a half a minute more.
3. Add in your lime juice, cabbage, coconut, carrots and olive oil, stirring to combine. Add the water, stirring well.
4. Lock the lid, and cook on high pressure for five minutes. Let the pressure naturally release for five minutes when you're done. After that five minutes use a quick pressure release.
5. Serve warm.

Sweet & Sour Red Cabbage

Ingredients:

- 3 Cups Cabbage
- ½ Cup Water
- ½ Cup applesauce
- ½ Tablespoon Apple Cider Vinegar
- 1 Tablespoon Chicken Broth
- ¼ Cup Onion, Minced
- 2 Cloves Garlic, Minced
- Sea Salt & Black Pepper to Taste

Directions:

1. Turn your instant pot to sauté, and then add in your broth and onion. Cook until they become transparent. Add in your garlic, sautéing for another minute. Stir often so that your garlic does not burn.
2. Add all other ingredients, and then close the lid. Cook on high pressure for ten minutes.
3. Use a quick release when done, and serve warm.

Dessert Recipes

Your instant pot can be used for dessert too! There's no reason that you can't have a great tasting desert made easy.

Cheesecake Bites

Ingredients:

Crust:

- 3-4 Graham Crackers, Ground Fine
- 2-3 Tablespoons Butter, Melted
- 1 Teaspoon Brown Sugar
- ¼ Cup All Purpose Flour

Mixture:

- 8 Ounces Cream Cheese, Room Temperature
- 1 Egg, Large & Room Temperature
- 1/6 Cup white Sugar
- ¼ Cup Sour Cream, Room Temperature
- 1 Tablespoon Cornstarch
- 1 Teaspoon Vanilla Extract
- Pinch of Sea Salt

Directions:

1. Mix your cheesecake batter together using a hand mixer. Do not use a stand mixer as they will overmix your cheesecake batter. To do this place your eggs, sour cream, cream cheese, and butter together. Mix well, but do not over mix.
2. In another bowl, mix your graham crackers and butter together. Add in a pinch of salt, your brown sugar and your flour. Mix well. Place your crust into the bottom of silicone baking cups. Freeze while you finish your cheesecake mixture.
3. Place your baking cups at 325 in the oven for twelve to fifteen minutes.

4. Beat your cornstarch, sea salt and sugar together before adding your cream cheese mixture.
5. Place into each cup after the crust is made.
6. Tap gently to remove air bubbles that would cause your cheesecake to split.
7. Add a cup of cold water to your instant pot, and then place your baking cups on the trivet. Close the lid, cooking for seven minutes with a natural pressure release when you're done.
8. Allow to cool before serving.

Egg Custard

Ingredients:

- ¾ Cup Whole Milk, Divided
- Sea Salt
- 2 Tablespoons White Sugar
- 2 Medium Eggs

Directions:

1. Add your sugar, sea salt and ½ cup of your whole milk into your pressure cooker. Melt your sugar, and use the slow cook function. Stir until your sugar is completely melted. Remove the pot, and let your milk cool.
2. Pour the remaining whole milk in, mixing well.
3. Beat your eggs in a measuring cup until well blended.
4. Slowly pour the milk mixture into your measuring cup while still mixing.
5. Strain the mixture through a fine mesh strainer twice, removing any solids.
6. Pour it into 2-3 ramekins, and remove air bubbles by tapping it gently with a spoon. Wrap them in aluminum foil tightly.
7. Pour a cup of your cold water into your instant pot, and then place the trivet in your instant pot. Set it to zero minutes and then a natural pressure release.
8. Serve warm.

White Wine & Vanilla Poached Pears

Ingredients:

- 1/2 Bottle White Wine
- ¾ Cup White Sugar
- 3-4 Small Pears, Firm but Ripe, Peeled
- ½ Cinnamon Stick, Broken in Half
- 1 Clove
- 1 Vanilla Bean Pod, Split Open Lengthwise
- ¼ Lemon, Cut into Round slices

Directions:

1. Add your sugar and wine to your instant pot, stirring until dissolved.
2. Add in your cinnamon stick, cloves, vanilla bean pod, lemon and pears.
3. Secure the lid, cooking on high pressure for eight minutes.
4. Use a natural pressure release, and then remove the pears. Place them to the side.
5. Remove the spices, and keep only two cups of liquid in your instant pot before hitting sauté. Cook until your sauce has reduced by half. This should take five to ten minutes.
6. Serve your pears drizzled with the sauce.

Poached Figs with Yogurt Crème

Ingredients:

Figs:

- ½ lb Figs
- ½ Cup Red Wine
- ¼ Cup Honey, Raw
- ¼ Cup Pine Nuts, Toasted

Yogurt Crème:

- 1 lb Yogurt

Directions:

1. Start by pouring your yogurt through a fine mesh strainer, and then place it in the coldest part of your fridge. Allow it to drain for two to three hours.
2. Add your wine to your instant pot, and then place your figs in the steaming basket.
3. Lock the lid, and cook on low pressure for three minutes.
4. Use a quick release.
5. Remove your figs, setting them to the side. Add your honey, and cook until your wine reduces by half.
6. Serve the sauce over your figs with a dollop of crème.

Stuffed Pears & Caramel Sauce

Ingredients:

- 1 Pear
- 1 ½ Tablespoons Butter, Divided
- 1/8 Cup Raisins
- ¼ Cup + 2 Tablespoons Water, Divided
- 1/8 Cup White Sugar
- 1/8 Cup Walnuts
- 1/8 Cup Rolled Oats
- ¼ Teaspoon Cinnamon
- ½ Teaspoon Vanilla Extract, Pure

Directions:

1. Cut your pears in half, and then scoop out the seeds.
2. Combine your butter, walnuts, raisins, cinnamon, oats and vanilla in a food processor. Pulse until you get a coarse meal. Divide among your pears.
3. Set your instant pot to sauté, and then add two tablespoons of water and your sugar. Stir to combine. Allow to cook while stirring occasionally until it turns a deep amber color. This will take about seven minutes. Add a half a cup of water, and stir well.
4. Arrange your pears on the caramel sauce, and then cook on low pressure for nine minutes.
5. Allow the pressure to release naturally for ten minutes, and then use a quick release for the rest. Remove the pears and set them to the side.
6. Put your instant pot on sauté, allowing your sauce to reduce for ten minutes.
7. Whisk a tablespoons of butter and your sea salt in.
8. Serve your pears drizzled with your caramel sauce.

Lavender Crème Brulee

Ingredients:

- 2 Egg Yolks
- 2/3 Cup Heavy Cream
- 2 Teaspoons Raw Sugar
- 2 Teaspoon Vanilla Extract, Pure
- Vanilla Beans, Scraped from Real Vanilla
- 1-1 ½ Teaspoons Food Grade Lavender Buds
- 2 Teaspoons Raw Sugar

Directions:

1. Warm your heavy cream, dissolving your sugar in it.
2. Whisk your cream mixture with your egg yolks. Add in your vanilla beans, lavender buds and vanilla extrac.t
3. Pour into two ramekins.
4. Add a cup of water into your instant pot before placing your trivet or steamer basket in. place your ramekins on top of the trivet.
5. Set on high for nine minutes, and then use a natural pressure release.
6. Take it out and let it cool for at least forty-five minutes. Refrigerate for an additional four to five hours.
7. Sprinkle a teaspoon of sugar on each, and broil until your sugar browns. This can take two to three minutes. Do not over broil or your crème will become softer.

Chocolate Bread Pudding

Ingredients:

- 1 Egg
- ¼ Cup Whole Milk
- ½ Teaspoon Cinnamon
- ¼ Cup Condensed Milk
- 2 Cups Challah Bread, Cubed
- 1/3 Cup Chocolate, Cut into Chunks
- 1 Cup Water

Directions:

1. Mix your milk, condensed milk, cinnamon and egg together in a bowl. Add your bread cubes and chocolate, stirring well. Gently divide between two ramekins.
2. Place the water in your instant pot before adding your trivet. Place your ramekins on the trivet, and then cover. Cook on high pressure for eleven minutes.
3. Serve while your pudding is still warm.

Fruit Cobbler

Ingredients:

- 1 Apple, Cored & Chopped
- 2 Tablespoons Honey, Raw
- 3 Tablespoons Coconut Oil
- 1 Pear, Cored & Chopped
- 1 Plum, Stone Removed & Chopped
- ¼ Cup Coconut, Shredded & Unsweetened
- ½ Teaspoon Cinnamon
- 2 Tablespoons Sunflower Seeds, Roasted
- ¼ Cup Pecans, Chopped

Directions:

1. In a bowl mix your plum, apple, pear, oil, cinnamon and honey. Stir, and then transfer to a metal baking pan. Steam for ten minutes in your instant pot before transferring to a bowl.
2. Put your sunflower seeds, coconut, and pecans in your drained instant pot. Press your sauté mode, cooking for five minutes. Sprinkle this over your fruit mixture.
3. Serve warm.

Black Rice Pudding

Ingredients:

- ½ Cup Black Rice, Rinsed
- ¾ Cup Water
- ½ Tablespoon Butter
- ¼ Teaspoon Sea Salt, Fine
- ¼ Cup Sugar
- ½ Cup Milk
- 2/3 Cup Half & Half
- ½ Teaspoon Vanilla Extract, Pure
- 1/3 Cup Cherries, Dried
- 1 Egg

Directions:

1. Combine your rice, butter, salt and water in your instant pot. Lock the lid, and cook on high pressure for twenty-two minutes.
2. Allow for a natural pressure release for ten minutes before using a quick release.
3. Add your milk and sugar, and then select the sauté button. Stir occasionally until your sugar has dissolved.
4. Whisk your eggs, half and half and vanilla together, and pour into a fine mess strainer. Strain into your instant pot, cooking while stirring constantly until it comes to a boil.
5. Turn off your instant pot and then stir in your cherries.
6. Serve warm or cold.

Chilled Fruit Soup

Ingredients:

- ¼ Cantaloupe, Rind Removed & Cut into Chunks
- 1 Small Orange, Peeled & Halved
- 8 ounces Pineapple Juice
- 1 Peach, Pit Removed
- 4 Ounces Greek Yogurt, Plain
- ¼ Teaspoon Vanilla Extract, Pure
- ½ Tablespoon Powdered Sugar
- ½ Tablespoons Chia Seeds

Directions:

1. Add your fruit and pineapple juice to your pressure cooker. Cook on high for five minutes before using a quick release.
2. Use an immersion blender, blending until you get a smooth puree.
3. Remove the pulp by pouring through a strainer.
4. Cool to room temperature before adding your Greek yogurt, powdered sugar and vanilla. Whisk To combine, and then chill.
5. Serve cold with chia seeds.

Chia Spiced Rice Pudding

Ingredients:

- ½ Cup Short Grain Rice
- ½ Cup Almond Milk, Unsweetened
- ½ Cup Coconut Milk, Unsweetened
- ½ + ¼ Cups Water
- 1 Tablespoon Brown Sugar
- 3 Medjool Dates, Sliced
- ½ Teaspoon Cinnamon
- ½ Teaspoon Ground Ginger
- ¼ Teaspoon Nutmeg
- 3 Cardamom Pods
- 1 Clove Allspice
- ½ Teaspoon Vanilla Extract, Pure

Directions:

1. Combine all of your ingredient into your instant pot, locking the lid. Cook on high pressure for ten minutes.
2. Allow for a natural pressure release for five minutes before using a quick release for the rest of the pressure
3. Open the lid, and stir.
4. Add more milk if you prefer it to be thinner, and top with nuts, seeds or dried fruit if desired.

Conclusion

Now you have everything you need to start your instant pot journey! There's no reason you can't use your instant pot to cook homemade and tasty meals for two. Soon enough you'll find that it's one of the most well used tools in your kitchen! There's no reason to deal with fast food which whole food can be made so simply and in half the time as opposed to using traditional cooking methods. Start your instant pot journey today, and explore the culinary delights that come with it.

Please get more tips and tricks on Instant Pot Cooking, Ketogenic cooking, and other fun and healthy ideas, please visit:
http://www.KetoDiet.coach

Also, if you have enjoyed this book, please leave me a review on Amazon. It will be greatly appreciated.

Sydney Foster

23388826R00093

Made in the USA
San Bernardino, CA
24 January 2019